THE JOWETT BRADFORD

My wife, Jane; daughter, Jessica; and grandsons, Oliver and Alex, standing next to my Bradford on a horrible wet day at the RNLI Flag Day in Whitby on 29 July 2018.

Jane and I with the Bradford on a much brighter day at Sleights Show on 16 August 2014.

THE JOWETT BRADFORD

JOWETT'S UNSUNG HERO

NOEL STOKOE

FONTHILL

Fonthill Media Language Policy

Fonthill Media publishes in the international English language market. One language edition is published worldwide. As there are minor differences in spelling and presentation, especially with regard to American English and British English, a policy is necessary to define which form of English to use. The Fonthill Policy is to use the form of English native to the author. Noel Stokoe was born and educated in York and now lives at Whitby, North Yorkshire; therefore British English has been adopted in this publication.

www.fonthillmedia.com
office@fonthillmedia.com

First published in the United Kingdom
and the United States of America 2019

British Library Cataloguing in Publication Data:
A catalogue record for this book is available from the British Library

Copyright © Noel Stokoe 2019

ISBN 978-1-78155-758-7

The right of Noel Stokoe to be identified as the author of this work has been asserted by him in accordance with the Copyright, Designs and Patents Act 1988.

All rights reserved. No part of this publication may be reproduced, stored in a retrieval system or transmitted in any form or by any means, electronic, mechanical, photocopying, recording or otherwise, without prior permission in writing from Fonthill Media Limited

Typeset in Minion Pro 10pt on 13pt
Printed and bound in England

CONTENTS

Introduction		7
1	History of the Jowett Bradford	9
2	Advertising the Bradford	24
3	Period Owners' Accounts of Bradford Ownership	31
4	Period Road Tests and Articles	40
5	Bradford Ownership Today	53
6	Bradfords in Museums around the World	120
7	A Selection of more Bradfords around Today	129
8	A Selection of Pictures Taken of Bradfords during 2018	135
Select Bibliography and Acknowledgements		142

This wonderful picture of a Bradford driving through Monk Bar in York registered KWF 776. The registration KWF is an East Yorkshire number that ran from March to September 1952, so it would age the Bradford at approximately August 1952. The car to the right, just behind the Bradford is a Standard 8 registered HGR 534, this was a Sunderland registration that ran from April 1957, this would date the picture at the end of 1957 at the earliest. (*Copyright The Francis Frith Collection— image reference number Y12044*)

Introduction

I HAVE WANTED TO write a book on the Jowett Bradford van for years, as I regard the Bradford as the unsung hero in the history of Jowett Cars Ltd. Back in the mid-1980s I took over as the publicity officer and librarian of the Jowett Car Club. At that time Jowett cars were often described as a 'Cinderella' make and received very little coverage in the 'old motor press'. Since then more and more publicity has come Jowett's way particularly in the case of the post-war Javelin and Jupiter, also vintage and pre-war models. I am very pleased to say that in recent years there has been a growing interest in the Bradford, which in my opinion is long overdue.

The Bradford was designed as a stop-gap model prior to the launch of the Javelin in 1947 but continued to be built right up to the closure of the company in 1954. As detailed later in this book, it was based on the 1938 8 hp commercial and was basically a pre-war design in every respect. It was, however, very popular with farmers and small businesses such as bakers, green grocers, fish mongers, drapers and sales reps etc. as it was economical, cheap, rugged and simple to work on.

Ironically, it was the largest selling model that Jowett ever produced in its 47-year car manufacturing history, producing almost 40,000 of them. It was the only post-war model to make a profit for the Jowett company. The profits from the sales of the Bradford partly funded the production costs of the Javelin and Jupiter—both of which lost money even though they were technically very advanced and ahead of their time. This could not be said of the Bradford, as it was already an eight-year-old design before its launch in 1946, receiving only minor improvements during its eight-year production run.

In my opinion, it is the ideal time to be recognising the Bradford, as over the last few years more and more interest is being shown on them. Many are now being restored from very poor condition which was not happening previously.

2018 was also a very special year for the Bradford, as over the early May bank holiday weekend the first ever rally exclusively for the Jowett Bradford was held. The Jowett Car Club has been holding international rallies annually since 1966 where all Jowetts, including Bradfords, are welcome, but this was the first time a rally had been arranged specifically for the Bradford. The three-day rally was based at a club member's hotel in Buxton and was a great success.

On the Saturday we visited the Steeple Grange light railway and the Ecclesbourne railway, both at Wirksworth followed by a scenic run to the National Tramway Museum at Crich on the Sunday. This reflects the increased interest in them and I am hoping it will now become a regular addition the club's calendar of events.

A Bradford, owned by the chairman and club's Bradford registrar, Paul Beaumont, has appeared on the club's stand at the Restoration Show at the NEC for the last four years. This show has only been running for four years and our stand has won 'the best working stand' every year! The Bradford first appeared as a 'barn find' wreck at the first show and has been worked on each show since. This year saw the fully restored chassis and mechanicals reassembled on the stand and was driven off as a working rolling chassis—next year's show will see the bodywork going back on!

A beautifully restored Bradford van also graced the Jowett stand at the prestigious Classic Car Show at the NEC in November 2013 which created a great deal of interest. In June this year a partially-restored Bradford lorry was displayed on the Jowett stand at the prestigious Bristol Classic Car Show, which also created a great deal of interest.

During 2018 several Bradfords have returned to the road after full restorations. I know of many more that are being restored at the moment, so should return to the road again in the future.

I wrote the above notes in September 2018 when the manuscript was submitted to the publishers which was probably the busiest year that the Bradford had ever experienced. At that time, I was hoping that there would be a second Bradford only rally in early May this year. I am pleased to say this has recently taken place and was another success, but the weather was not as kind this year! The Jowett Car Club international rally was also held over the late May Bank Holiday weekend and the Bradford was well represented again with fourteen entered. I can also report that several new 'barn-find' Bradfords have already turned up this year which we hope will be restored.

The future certainly looks bright for the Bradford which is finally being properly recognised.

Noel Stokoe
May 2019

1

HISTORY OF THE BRADFORD

N 1942 JOWETT Cars Ltd started making plans for the production of new post-war car models; these would need to be all-new, and suitable for the world market. Jowett engaged the services of a young engineer named Gerald Palmer, who had previously worked for the Nuffield Group. He was given a small office, and basically a blank canvas as regard to its design. He had been working with Issigonis, who would go on to build the Morris Minor, and later, the Mini. His first prototype Minor was known as the Mosquito and was built with a horizontally-opposed flat-four engine, but this was dropped in favour of a conventional four-cylinder in-line side-valve engine which had already been in production in the pre-war Morris 8. Gerald also wanted to use a flat-four engine in his new car design, but he had no problem obtaining permission to use it, as it was carrying on the tradition of using a horizontally-opposed design that the Jowett brothers had used since their first prototype car in 1906. The new car would be the sensational Javelin saloon, but Jowetts needed something to sell, while work on the Javelin was taking place.

At the end of the Second World War in 1945 Britain had massive debts and the Government watchword was export, export, export! All raw materials such as aluminium, steel and seasoned timber were all in very short supply, and car manufacturers had to export to qualify for receiving them.

At this time Jowett Cars Ltd also bought a little showroom at 48 Albemarle Street, London, which was just off Piccadilly. The showroom was run by John Baldwin, who had served during the war in the RAF. Prior to this he had been employed by an American soap company. One of his main duties was publicity and advertising. He hit on the idea of placing adverts in newspapers, asking for readers' opinions as to the type of commercial vehicle Jowetts should be producing. This came about as he was embarrassed by the fact that the showroom only had the 1913 tiller-steered Jowett and a wooden model of the

Above and below: Two views of the pre-war Jowett 8 hp Jowett van which was the basis of the post-war Bradford van. It is quite clear from these pictures that very little changed design-wise, the most noticeable changes being the radiator cowl and the wheels. This vehicle was registered CAK 756 which was a Bradford registration from October 1937. These pictures must have been taken towards the end of the Second World War as it is advertising the post-war Javelin. The designer, Gerald Palmer, only joined Jowett's in 1942 to start work on designing the Javelin. (*JCC Archive*)

This is the picture used in the first sales booklet that was produced for the Bradford in December 1945; this was clearly an early mock-up of what the Bradford was to look like. As mentioned above, when production started it had a different radiator cowl and wheels. The sales booklets must have been produced before the first Bradfords rolled off the production line, but I assume they felt there was no point wasting them! (*JCC Archive*)

Thanet Electronics was a radio and television shop which operated from 1947 to 1973 in Cliftonville, Margate, Kent, it was owned by Alan's father and a business partner. In the early days of the business they ran three Bradfords, this being one of them. (*Alan Rushworth*)

Javelin in it. This proved to be incredibly successful, as an advert in a Saturday issue of the *Daily Express* produced over 3,000 replies the following Monday! There were replies from people from all walks of life, but in particular, from farmers and small business owners who wanted a simple light commercial, and more than half of the farmers wanted light lorries.

The Javelin was not expected to be available for at least two years, so it was therefore agreed to re-vamp the 1938 8 hp commercial as it was simple and cheap to build, and it was expected to sell well. Gerald Palmer had thought that the whole front end of this model should be re-designed to make its appearance a little more modern, but this did not happen. The chassis was the same as the 1938–1940 models, but there were various body-work alterations suggested by Briggs to simplify the production process and reduce costs.

The original grille mock-up had the word *Bradford* written horizontally across it, and not *Jowett*, that had graced all pre-war models. This grille design featured on the early sales literature but was changed on the final design to the top centre of the radiator cowl, where the wording was altered to *Bradford by Jowett*. It was thought by many that the new model was known as the Bradford, so prospective buyers would know where it had been built. Another school of thought was that the Jowett company was rather embarrassed to put their name to such an antiquated vehicle in this brave new post-war world!

When Charles Callcott-Rielly was appointed by Jowett in 1939 he dismantled the old pre-war production lines to make way for the new equipment required for going into war production. He had the old equipment removed to enable a modern conveyor system and a new assembly shop. This bold project was undertaken by Frank Slater, who had done a similar job for The Standard Motor Company Limited works before the war. The thinking behind these improved production lines was that when the war was over, it would allow them to build better vehicles than many of their competitors who would still be relying on pre-war production methods.

A decision had already been taken that bodies would no longer be built in-house; they would be supplied by Briggs of Dagenham. Briggs also built a plant at Doncaster, which would be ideal for Jowetts as it was only 30 miles away from the Jowett factory. Their job numbers were 48 for the Javelin and 49 for the Bradford. In the case of the Bradford, they placed a small brass plate on the bulkhead with the job number (49) followed by a letter, to denote the body type:–

49A—The Van body
49B—The drive-away chassis front-end
49C—Chassis frame and chassis parts
49D—The Cab
49E—The Float—(the flatbed of a lorry)
49F—The Six-Light Utility
49G—The Utility Deluxe
49H—The Four-Light Utility

A sales booklet on the Bradford was available by December 1945, and by early 1946 production was underway. The first design was known as the CA, and was originally only available in van form, but by June a lorry version was introduced. Due to John Baldwin's efforts, demand was high for the new model and waiting lists continued to grow, as potential owners desperately wanted to get their hands on one.

When production of the Bradford got underway a new system of four production lines was used. The first line made the engines, which were, of course, the twin-cylinder horizontally-opposed engine of 1,005 cc which produced a maximum of 19 bhp at 3,500 rpm. This was the continuation of the pre-war *little engine with the big pull*. Starting from the opposite end and in line with the engine line, the three-speed gearbox was assembled. When the engines were completed they were moved to a test-bed where they were turned over by an electric motor and then the engine was run properly and tested. When the engine was accepted it was attached to a gearbox. The engine and gearbox lines met in the middle, so it was a simple procedure to marry the two units together.

The production line for the body ran parallel to the engine line where iron sub-frames were used to carry the Briggs body parts which used aluminium sheet sides fastened to an ash frame. It was then fitted with steel doors and a heavy-duty fabric roof. As the bodies moved along the production line they were fitted with electrical parts, the wooden floor, wings and internal and external fittings. Originally the Briggs components would have come from the main plant in Dagenham, but after their new plant was opened in Doncaster, most came from there.

The main chassis assembly line ran parallel to these lines. On this line the chassis frame was built, the front and rear axles were fitted, the steering gear was added and so were brake fittings. The combined engine/gearbox was then lifted on and fitted, followed by the body. All connections were made, wheels, front wings and bumper, and a driver's seat were fitted, (it should be remembered that a passenger seat was an optional extra at £4 0s 0d!) When everything was in place the engine was started and tested again. All electrical functions were then tested and adjusted.

The finished vehicle was then driven off the line, fitted with trade plates, supplied with a small amount of fuel and taken for a road test. When it returned to the assembly area any faults were notified to the Rectification Department and once these had been corrected the vehicle was driven to the Wash Bay, where it was cleaned and polished. They were then taken to the Delivery & Collection Bay for drivers to take them to UK Jowett Agents, or the docks around the country for export.

This new model was described in *The Commercial Motor* from 6 July 1945 under the heading:

A 1949 Bradford towing a Thomson Kelvin Star caravan, the driver, Norris Bridgens, received a 15-minute telling off from an AA Scout for attempting to climb the 1 in 4 Porlock Hill and getting stuck part-way up. He complained that he was balked by another car that had already run into difficulty! (*The Caravan Club*)

An interesting high-sided Bradford being used by the Paragon Laundry of Handsworth. This body will have been built by a local coachbuilder on a rolling chassis provided by Jowett's. (*JCC Archive*)

Albert Harrison & Co. Ltd of Accrington, Lancashire was founded in 1919 and is still in business today. They specialise in wholesale distribution of products including confectionery, health & beauty and stationery across the UK. This photograph, taken in the 1950s shows some of their fleet of vehicles, including three Bradford vans. (*Harrison*)

Joy's of Selby were poultry breeders and this picture shows some of the fleet of commercial vehicles that they owned in the 1950s, which included a Bradford van and Bradford Utility. (*David Joy*)

New Jowett available as a Van or Lorry

Stronger chassis frame and redesigned van body are two features of the new Jowett models which have just been announced. The Jowett commercial vehicle is distinctive in that it is the only example on the British market employing a two cylindered horizontally opposed engine. The maker, Jowett Cars, Ltd., Idle, Bradford, announces that two models are available, one an 8-cwt. van and the other a 10-cwt. lorry, both of which sell at £260.

The chassis specification is identical to both models, with the exception that the suspension on the lorry is somewhat stiffer. On request, the van can be similarly equipped. Engine, clutch and gearbox are of unit construction, being three-point mounted on rubber in the frame. The cylinder bore is 79.4 mm and the piston stroke 101.6 mm.

A single dry-plate clutch takes the drive to a three-speed-and-reverse gearbox, providing overall ratios of 18.1 to 1 (1st) 9.3 to 1 (2nd) and 4.89 to 1 (3rd) and 24.7 to 1 reverse.

A pressed-steel banjo-type rear axle is employed, in which the axle shafts are semi-floating and the final drive by spiral-bevel gear. Semi-elliptic springs, in conjunction with Luvax hydraulic shock absorbers, are used for suspension, the wheels being of the 'ventilated' disc type and equipped with 17 by 4.30 Goodyear tyres.

An entirely new design of frame employs side members of a deep box-section, which are extended to the rear of the body platform cross-members are tubular; and the whole structure has been designed to withstand whip and to reduce roll on corners-to a minimum.

Braking is by mechanical actuation, the equipment being of Bendix Cowdrey make with self-servo-type shoes. Lighting, starting and coil ignition current is supplied by a 6-volt battery carried under the bonnet.

The maximum inside width of the van body is 4 ft. 8 ins., whilst it is 4 ft. 7 ins. long behind the seat with a maximum inside length of 8 ft, 6 ins., In the case of the lorry body, the platform measures 5 ft. 6 ins, by 4 ft. 11 ins. Steering is by Bishop cam gear and the vehicle can be turned in a 34-ft. circle.

Another interesting note that appeared in *The Commercial Motor* from 24 January 1947 stating that Bradfords were to be built in India:

A £100,000 factory near Bombay is planned by Motor House (Gujarat), Ltd., which assembles and distributes Jowett vehicles, and handles American vehicles made by the Henry Kaiser organization. From the Bradford works of Jowett Cars, Ltd., vehicle components have been leaving for India since last spring, and Bradford commercial vehicles are already being marketed there.

I have not, as yet, been able to find out if the production of Bradfords ever took place, and if they did, how many were made.

HISTORY OF THE JOWETT BRADFORD

According to *The Commercial Motor* dated 4 April 1947:

'Bradford vehicles have been exported to over 70 countries, from China in the east to Vancouver in the west, and from Cape Town in the south to Iceland in the north', said Mr. Charles Clore, chairman of Jowett Cars, Ltd., at the company's annual general meeting. 'Orders had been received from overseas for 9,000 Bradfords, apart from heavy commitments in the home market.

So, we know that Bradfords were exported to at least 70 countries; some are obvious, such as Australia, New Zealand, Europe, Canada, plus South American countries, such as Argentina and Brazil. We do know, however, that Javelins were exported to 81 countries, so I personally think this figure is closer to the mark for the Bradford.

During 1946 Briggs supplied Jowetts with 3,434 van bodies, 430 drive-away chassis front-ends and over 200 cabs and floats. By the end of 1948 the total had increased to 11,885 van bodies, 1,770 chassis, 2,736 standard utilities, 1,590 de-luxe utilities and over 1,000 cabs and floats.

The second series Bradford known as the CB was built in 1947 after having built approximately 5,000 of the earlier CA model. It was still the same basic design, with the 1,005 cc engine. The engine now had a down-draught carburettor fitted, and a belt driven dynamo, which allowed a cooling fan to be fitted for the first time. This was an optional extra, but proved popular in export vehicles going to hotter countries such as Australia, New Zealand, Brazil and Uruguay.

It also continued to be a successful export model for Jowett with *The Commercial Motor* from 12 March 1948 stating that:

'Last year 35 per cent. of the output of Bradford vans was exported', says Mr. George Wansbrough, Chairman of Jowett Cars, Ltd., in a statement to be read at the annual general meeting on 15th March. He states that, 'In the national interest, sales in the home market should be increased. For the first eight weeks of this year, markets which could absorb hundreds of vehicles were closed to us. If these markets can be reopened and kept open, we can hope to export our full quota. If the effect of Government action is to reduce our total van production, costs will inevitably rise, and it will be difficult, and may even be impossible, to export more than a small proportion of our potential van production'.

The Commercial Motor from 25 June 1948 stated that:

An order for 200 Bradford 8 hp utility vehicles for Spain has been received by Jowett Cars, Ltd through Aravix Motors, Ltd. Fifty have already been shipped and the remainder will be dispatched in a few days in MV *Pelayo*. The whole of the space in this vessel has been chartered for the shipment.

The CB model continued in production into late 1949 when the third series Bradford CC was introduced. The engine was completely redesigned with the new RAC rating increasing from 19 bhp to 25 bhp. The electrics were finally also altered from a 6-volt to a 12-volt system. This was not before time as Jowetts received many complaints due to the inadequacy of the 6-volt system, when customers literally ran out of power on dark and wet nights when headlights and wipers were in operation at the same time!

There were various utility vehicles produced during production of the Bradford van from 1946 onwards, as well as pick-up lorries. The utilities typically had six seats, with side windows and with larger rectangular windows in the rear doors, although various versions were made with optional rear seats, depending on the vagaries of purchase tax during this period. Many of the Bradfords were supplied as a drive-away chassis so that customers could have special bodies fitted.

A memo produced by Briggs which listed the non-Fords produced by them between 1946 and 1953, the Bradford totalled 4,280 in 1946, 7,229 in 1947, 8,920 in 1948, 6,095 in 1949, 3,558 in 1950, 3,576 in 1951, 4,444 in 1952 and 139 in 1953. This came to a grand total of 38,241, but it is not clear if this figure included the CKD figure (Complete Knock Downs) which were exported in large numbers, particularly to Australia and New Zealand. The engine design was basically the same as the first car designed by the brothers in the 1906 prototype car, a production run of over 47 years.

Several local authorities bought Bradford vans for use in the library service, this example was used by Sheffield Library in the 1950s. (*Sheffield CC*)

The lord mayor of Bradford witnesses the 10,000th Bradford rolling off the production line, this one is destined for India. (*Telegraph & Argus, Bradford*)

This excellent picture of a Bradford lorry transporting two pianos was spotted by a club member on what we think was a Russian website. After a bit of research, we were able to confirm the picture was taken in Melbourne, Australia in the 1950s.

At this stage I must mention that the Bradford that we know, and love should have been replaced, in 1951 by the all-new CD range, but sadly, never was. I covered the CD project in my book *Jowett 1901–1954* and it is covered in much more detail in *Jowett–The Complete History* by Paul Clark & Ed Nankivell, but I feel I should mention it again briefly here, as the story is not complete without it.

In March 1949 Jowett realised that the Bradford needed updating or replacing by the launch of the all-new post-war Bradford range of vehicles.

The design work for the new Bradford was given to Briggs, as the Javelin had proved expensive to build. It was felt that Briggs that would be able to produce a less complicated and cheaper design, with mass production in mind.

In March 1950 Charles Grandfield carried out a complete policy review and did not like what he saw; in his view the Javelin was too noisy and unreliable, the Bradford was too old fashioned and with a too-small pay load area, and the Jupiter which was totally untested. His proposals for the future were set out as follows:–

1 Modify the Javelin in two stages. Stage 1 for the October '51 Motor Show would be minor body changes with engine improvements to increase reliability and reduce noise. Stage 2 would be ready for the following year's Motor Show, which would include a new flat four engine 90 mm × 90 mm giving 2¼ litres.

2 Design changes to the Jupiter on an ongoing basis, as and when more was known about the car.

3 The CD commercial to be developed in two stages, Stage 1 for the October Motor Show of 1951. Stage 2 known as the CE commercial would be ready for the 1952 Show and would also use the new 2¼-litre Javelin engine.

As the CD project developed it was proposed that a full range of models should be produced, van, estate, pick-up and car, all pressings would only differ from behind the front door pillar. It was felt that a cheap car would be a success, as more first-time car owners took to the road each year. If it had been a success, there was even talk of dropping the Javelin, without a replacement. By the end of 1950 Jowett produced the first CD prototype known as 'the tram' in its experimental department and was tested extensively over the next 12 months.

Briggs was tooling up production lines for the new range and pushing Jowett for firm orders. Jowett in turn was having problems with Javelin unreliability such as broken crankshafts, and the 'in house' gearbox fiasco and was not able to make such commitments. During 1951 tooling costs kept increasing but by December the first prototype van was delivered—registered HKW 272, six months late! In May 1952 an order for 2,500 vans, 1,250 pick-ups and 1,250 station wagons was finally placed. The following month, the rather stylish pick-up prototype was received and registered HKY 566. The only car produced by Briggs was received in July 1953 and registered JKU 399.

The sad fact was that mechanical problems with the Javelin, increased tooling costs, delays, and lack of finance resulted in the CD range never going into production. Only one car, one pick-up, and around eight van/estates were built in prototype form. Three estates survive in New Zealand, and one in this country, sadly the car and pick-up were both scrapped.

As mentioned several times before, the Bradford was basically a pre-war design in all respects, which was meant as a short-term model prior to the launch of the Javelin. It was a reliable, uncomplicated, frugal workhorse in the true Jowett brothers' tradition. It was loved by shopkeepers, small business owners and the general public alike. Ironically, this was the only profitable model Jowett produced in the post-war period. It was also the most successful model that Jowetts produced either pre-war or post-war, with almost 40,000 of them being built. Profits generated from this model were used in the development and launch of the more glamorous Javelin and Jupiter, both of which were never successful.

The CD Bradford estate and the CD pick-up just visible behind, they were used by Jowett Engineering Ltd at Howden Clough as their daily transport until it closed down in 1964. (*JCC Archive*)

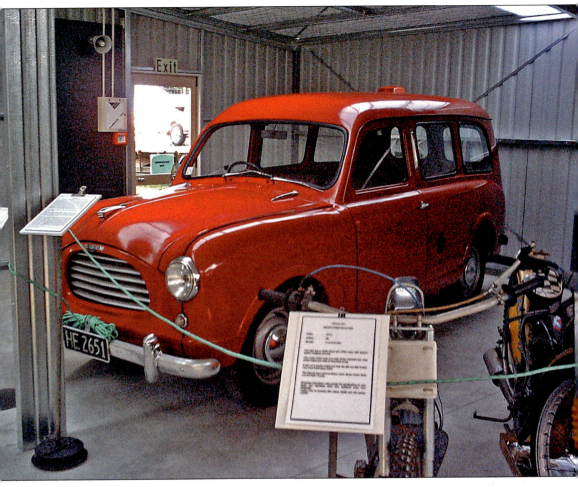

The only restored CD Estate at the moment is in the Win Collection in New Zealand, this is a fantastic collection of Jowetts, which is described in more detail later in the book. (*Eden Lindsay*)

Opposite above: The CD car was also in service with Jowett Engineering, but sadly was scrapped when they closed down in 1964. (*JCC Archive*)

Opposite below: A later shot of the CD estate taken in the 1970s, this vehicle has survived and is in the process of a lengthy restoration. (*JCC Archive*)

2

ADVERTISING THE BRADFORD

THE FIRST SALES booklet for the Bradford appeared in December 1945, and like everything else connected with the Bradford, it was rather low-key. It was a large single sheet folded in two to produce four sides in approximately A4 size. The outer cover had a side-view of the Bradford showing its front-half on the front and its rear carried across onto the rear cover. Inside there were two pictures of the van, a three-quarter front view and a front view. There was also a side view of the lorry. The inside two sides had details of the 10 cwt Bradford Van in grey primer, ex-works, at £255 0s 0d and the 10 cwt Lorry at £255 0s 0d.

Clearly, this brochure was produced prior to the vehicles being available, as the pictures on the front cover and inside show a mock-up of the van and lorry with a different grille to the one on the production models. Other notable differences were that there was no front bumper, there were twelve holes in the artillery wheels, which later became fifteen, there were also different bonnet catches and trafficators lower down the body side. Side lights were also fitted to the front wings but disappeared on the later production models. This is the information that was quoted in the sales brochure:

Features of the Bradford 10 cwt Van

Capacity—Biggest Body Capacity—89 Cubic Feet
Economy—Highest Pay-Load (8–10 cwt) with lowest fuel and maintenance Costs, 35 mpg with average loads.
Reliability—Assured by the simple Balanced Power principle in Engine Design
Strength—Chassis specially evolved for Commercial Work

ADVERTISING THE BRADFORD

Biggest body capacity. That means more work from each vehicle you use. Lowest unladen weight for the payload you get. That means greater economy of running—you don't waste pulling power on weight that is not being put to use in the shape of goods carried. Equipment modern and complete. New design of body and chassis based on findings of many years' experience in building commercial vehicles. All these you will have in the Bradford commercial. You will also have the "Balanced Power" of Jowett's unique horizontally opposed engine. And that means economy, sturdy pulling, smooth performance and, above all, reliability. The simple "Balanced Power" principle has established for Jowett a reputation for reliability that has probably never been equalled, and certainly never surpassed, in the light commercial class.

Low maintenance costs ensured by low-speed 2-cylinder side valve engine of simple construction with few moving parts and having good pulling power at low speeds. Low piston and bearing speeds mean less wear.

Simple 3-speed gearbox of robust proportions "Lay-Rub" propeller shaft needing no lubrication. Sturdy box-sectioned frame with tubular cross-members and strongly constructed body give great road stability. Softer springs can be provided for vehicles handling light bulky loads.

Bendix Cowdrey self-servo brakes, Bishop Cam steering, very light control—34 feet turning circle, easily manoeuvrable easy-clean wheels and heavy duty tyres.

A virtually identical brochure appeared in May 1946, the outside cover is identical to the previous one with the side-view of the Bradford, still with the wrong grille. Inside there was a new three-quarter front view of the van with the correct Bradford grille, but surprisingly, the original side-view of the lorry remained the same with the mock-up grille. The above information published in the first brochure remained with identical wording. The *Motor* magazine of 7 August 1946 quoted, 'Jowett announce at Bradford six-seater Utility', this was reproduced as a single-sided flier measuring 8 inches × 6 inches to advertise the model. There were two pictures of a Six-Light Utility, one from the rear with the back doors open and a three-quarter view from the rear.

These two pictures were reproduced again in a single sheet flier headed 'Now!—A Six-Seater Bradford Utility by Jowett' measuring 8½ inches × 7 inches. The text on the front read:

A six-seater Utility has been introduced on the famous Jowett Bradford 8 hp chassis, to provide roomy accommodation for six as a station-wagon or shooting brake whilst retaining all the advantages of a capacious van for carrying normal goods or luggage on occasion.

The dimensions of the six-seater Utility are the same as those of the Bradford van, giving 93 cubic feet with an 8 cwt payload. The economical two-cylinder engine gives a petrol consumption of over 40 mph with normal loads. The standard specification includes six seats (four easily removable), front bumper, choice of grey, blue or green finish, and a spare wheel. Price ex-works £320.

The rear of the flier lists the model types and prices:

Vehicles
Bradford Van (Ex-Works) £280
Bradford Lorry (Ex-Works) £280
Bradford Cab Chassis (Ex-Works) £265
Bradford Drive-Away Chassis (Ex-Works) £235
Bradford Six-Seater Utility (Ex-Works) £320
Extras on Vans and Lorries
Passenger Seat £4
Painting in one of the three colours, Grey, Blue or Green £8
Extras on Chassis
Driver's Seat   £4
Additional Seat £4
Pair of Doors £15

The next sales booklet—produced in February 1947—was in yellow and white, it was a single sheet (approximately A3 size) folded in half to make four sides. There is a front-view of a Bradford on the front and has this heading, *The Bradford 10 cwt Van—Lorry—Six-Seater Utility* and the inside pages have the same pictures of a van, six-light and the lorry, with the following text:

When the Jowett factory at Idle, Bradford, Yorkshire, had finished its War work, immediate steps were taken to put into production again a range of light commercial vehicles. These are now known as the Bradford range which consists of the 10 cwt Van, the drop-side Lorry, the six-seater Utility and six-light Van, together with a deluxe range consisting of the Van and Utility.

The Bradford chassis follows the general lines of the well-known pre-war models (many of which have done 250,000 miles and more), but it has been considerably strengthened and the water-cooled horizontally opposed twin-cylinder engine has been redesigned to give a greater power output. Now rated at 8 hp, this 1005 cc unit develops 19 bhp at 3,500 rpm, and is notable for its solid construction and simplicity, its hard-working qualities and the high-power output at low engine speeds. Owing to the big bearing surfaces and the fewer moving parts which this flat twin design permits, longer life, greater economy and consistent reliability are ensured.

The Jowett factory has been producing horizontally opposed water-cooled twins since 1906 and, as the testing ground is the wild country of the Yorkshire Moors, a very hardy vehicle has been developed, suitable for use in any part of the world. The Bradford has already won a permanent overseas market and is backed by a world-wide spares service.

The Bradford Six-Seater Utility or Six-Light Van, Economy, Long Life, Big Loads, Reliability, Simplicity, Strength

The leaflet for the deluxe models was also in white and yellow and measured approximately A4 in size, it was a double-sided single sheet with a side-view black and white photo of a Utility De Luxe on the front, with two photos of the interior on the rear. There is also a quote on the back of the leaflet taken from *The Motor* dated 29 January 1947, which reads:

> The slogging power of this engine is exceptional, and, in fact, is one of the most satisfactory things about the whole vehicle. There is a kind of tenacity which enables long, steep climbs to be made without the need of changing down, and, alternatively, the degree of acceleration and the general power made available by intelligent use of the three-speed gear-box is a further factor which does this car much credit.
>
> Perhaps the most surprising feature of the whole chassis is the steering which is very light and requires rather less than two turns of the wheel from lock to lock, in spite of an exceptional turning circle of 34 feet. It is in fact, a form of steering which would do credit to a full-scale sporting car.
>
> Price Ex-Works in Beige Cellulose, Utility £415 plus £115 0s 6d Purchase Tax, Van £410.

The sales brochure from November 1949 is very similar to the one from February 1947, except that it has a green and white front cover, approximately A4 in size and folds out into six sides. This one also has the same front-view of a van, with the heading, *The 4 Famous Bradfords—Jowett*. The front number plate reads JCL 1949. Inside there is a picture and short write-up of each of the four models: the 10 cwt Van, Van or Utility Deluxe, 4-Light Van or Utility and the 10 cwt Lorry.

> Prices as at 11 November 1949
>
> 10 cwt Van—in Primer £335, painted £343
>
> Deluxe Van—in Cellulose £410 plus purchase tax of £116 0s 7d
>
> 4-Light Van—in Primer £349 10s, painted £357 10s
>
> 10 cwt Lorry—in Primer £325, painted £333
>
> Drive-Away Chassis (export only at present) £265

The last sales brochure I have seen was dated February 1952, and is smaller than the previous ones, measuring 23.5 cm high and 18.5 cm wide. It too is entitled *4 Famous Bradfords by Jowett of Bradford*. There are side-view drawings in orange against a grey background of the four models: the 10 cwt Van, Utility Deluxe, The 4-Light Van or Utility and the 10 cwt Lorry.

It is very interesting to me to see that this brochure still relies very heavily on Jowetts pre-war history, considering that by this time the Bradford had been in production for well over six years:

Here are the four famous Bradfords which Jowetts of Idle, Bradford, Yorkshire, are building; the 10 cwt Van, the drop-side Lorry, the six-seater Utility and the Utility deluxe. Both Utilities are available without rear seats, but otherwise to the same specification, as 4-Light vans. Bradfords have made a great reputation in the commercial field since the war, continuing to offer sturdy enduring vehicles which can be run at the lowest possible running cost. The basic design of a horizontally opposed, water cooled, four-stroke, twin cylinder unit was first introduced by Jowetts in 1906, so nearly 50 years of development have gone into these sturdy Yorkshire vehicles. The declared policy of incorporating developments when proved, rather than changing details each season, is continued, and thus the latest CC type models have only detail alterations as compared with their highly successful predecessors, the CA, and CB, these new features including 12-volt electrical equipment.

Stronger Chassis—The Bradford chassis follows the general design of the well-known pre-war models but have been considerably strengthened to take the normal wear and tear of a commercial vehicle. The vans and lorry have 10 cwt springs and the utilities 8 cwt.

More Power—Here is a big stride forward. The engine, which has always been one of the sturdiest and most economical in the world, has been modified to include all the experience gained since the war in many markets. The horizontally opposed twin cylinder water cooled 1,005 cc engine still has a nominal rating of 8 hp but develops 25 bhp at 3,500 rpm, an increase of 6 bhp. The power is now transmitted through a Borg & Beck clutch and a 3-speed synchromesh easy change gearbox. Bigger bearing surfaces promote even longer life. And, of course, the fewer, sturdier moving parts mean easy maintenance and provide the capacity this engine has for hard slogging under all conditions all over the world.

Special Purposes—For special body purposes the Bradford chassis can be supplied either as a "drive-away" chassis (fitted with a temporary box seat) or as a "cab" chassis which has a cab fitting complete and is ready for the body-building behind the cab. At present the chassis is not available on the home market.

Export Models—All Bradfords are available with left-hand steering and metric instruments for export. Overseas Bradfords are fitted with export air cleaners.

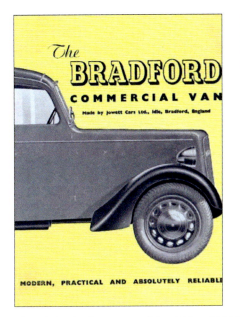

Above left: The front cover of the 1945 and 1946 sales booklet.

Above right: The front cover of the 1947 sales booklet.

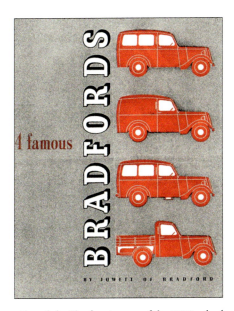

Above left: The front cover of the 1952 sales booklet.

Above right: A sales booklet produced by Liberty Motors of Melbourne, Australia showing a Bradford special with bodywork of their own design. It is exactly the same as the Bradford which was owned by the late Beryl Langley featured in the Owner's of Today section. (*Michael Allfrey*)

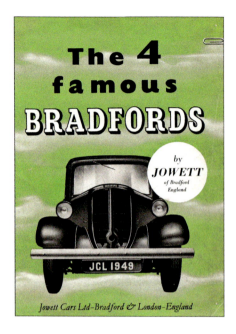
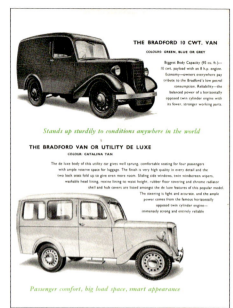
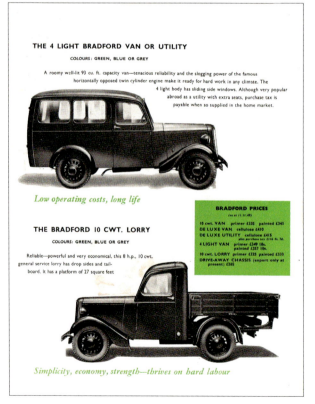

The front cover and two pages taken from the 1949 sales booklet.

3

Period Owners of Bradfords

Bradford Registered ACN 234

I have been shown the Jowett story in the *Darlington & Stockton Times* dated 28 Dec 2012. My first car was a Jowett Bradford van with side windows and a bus seat in the back which I bought in 1959. It cost me £40 and I owned it for about two years. It taught me a lot about driving with the crash gearbox which was the other way around to all other cars of the time and the Girling rod brakes which needed notice in writing to stop the car. The starter ring was shot so I had to hand start it every time. It was very hard to stop the oil leaks from the valve spring covers. I also had to change one of the cylinders which developed a crack in the bore. Having said the above, I do not regret owning the car as it improved my driving and maintenance skills and to this day I still keep a very safe distance from the car in front. Please note the large headlamps that I fitted to the van.

The number plate is still in the loft. I hope this is of interest to you.

Regards, John Lowe
10 February 2013

ACN 234 was a Bradford van that had windows cut into the sides (the small oval van windows in the rear doors are still visible) and was bought by John Lowe in 1959 for £40, he ran for two years. Note the large non-standard headlamps! (*J. Lowe*)

Bradford Registered OTD 328

I bought my blue and black Bradford van registration number OTD 328 from a friend of mine a week after he bought it from Jack Penswick's Garage in Pressall. The reason why he re-sold it was because he was unable to change gear in it as the box was so worn that the synchro on the top gears had gone. He gave £10 for it in 1963 and I bought it from him a week later for £8. I had known the van for years as it belonged to the local butcher in Knott End called Jack Price, for whom I had done a Saturday morning meat round on a delivery bike in my early teenage years. He was a heavy smoker and left lit Capstan Full Strength cigs everywhere, so this was my early introduction to smoking. My friend had taken the van back to the garage and complained, but to no avail. I was at college in Birmingham at the time, so it travelled regularly between Knott End and the college at weekends. My education grant did not amount to much at the time, so things had to go to put fuel in the tank even though it was about four gallons for £1 at the local Jet garage. I think my record player was sold, the golf clubs went (I had been a junior champion at Knott End Golf Club) and anything else I could sell to remain mobile. I also worked during the Christmas period doing the Christmas mail to bring in extra cash.

I needed one and a half lanes to keep it going in a straight-ish line at full chat. Maintenance was done on an *ad-hoc* basis, but it was tinkered with out of curiosity with few tools and

Period Owners' Accounts of Bradford Ownership

even less knowledge. I had previously owned a half share in a Standard Flying 12 and a Tiger 70 motorcycle, but still had much to learn. On one occasion I was working on the van in Birmingham with the exhaust removed, later I moved the vehicle without thinking, the outcome was one badly bent exhaust system, which I had run over, which had to go to a local blacksmith for some TLC and made to fit again.

I am not sure of its fuel consumption, but it used a pint of oil every 80 miles! This was probably due to the stop/starting on the meat round whilst his wife looked after the shop. I was under the impression that the thicker the oil would result in less oil being used, I was told that this was not the case, so I simply kept a watchful eye on the oil level and carried a spare gallon can when going some distance.

A failing battery and lack of funds usually made me park the Bradford on an incline to make life easier or enlist the aid of a helper to push-start it. On one occasion whilst visiting a relative I had to get my uncle drafted in to push.

On a visit to Denton I parked in the local square and was approached by a chap offering me a complete van, less the body. I said I was a penniless student and didn't need spare parts, but he was very persuasive, and I finally caved in and agreed to pay £5.00 for them. I told him that I had little money on me but would pay for them as and when. I collected the parts the next day and paid him what I could spare, which I think, was about £1.00 as I needed fuel to get back to Birmingham. The balance took me a month or three to settle. It was fortunate that I had got the parts as it was very cold that winter. I remember I had returned to Knotts End for Christmas and had forgotten to drain the system that night because there was no anti-freeze in it. Core plugs did not come into it—there was a huge piece blown out of the near-side cylinder water jacket. The new engine was then fitted as the result with a bit of difficulty as the steering column was in the way. Anyway, it was a really good engine and there was no need to constantly leave a smokescreen or carry a gallon of oil when I was out and about.

Whilst at college we used to visit girl's colleges for Saturday night dances and so on, one Sunday morning I was returning and went through a police radar trap—two police constables and a sergeant pulled me over saying I was speeding. I protested my innocence saying that this old van with two cylinders going uphill was not capable of speeding. I was let off the speeding offence, but I was still given a ticket as the handbrake was very poor and jamming my boot under the wheel whilst the bobbies were pushing it was never going to work! The fine, as I recall, was 15 shillings, which was a lot of Worthington E beer at the time!

I do not recall when it was sold, but I decided to call it a day when my indicators failed and my electrical knowledge, and that of my friends, was unable to fix them for the MOT, so it was sold for £30.00 and I bought a Sunbeam 58 motorcycle instead.

Regards Dave Millward,
Horwich, Bolton, March 2013

OTD 328 was bought in 1963 by Dave Millward for the knock-down price of £8 as the previous owner (a friend of his) could not start it. Needless to say, Dave got it going and ran it for several years then sold it for £30! (*D. Millward*)

Bradford Registered PNK 836

An acquaintance of mine, Ken Maddison, recently lent me a copy of your book *Jowett—A Century of Memories* as he knows of my interest in Jowetts (he is a member of the Jowett Car Club and his daughter is the Membership Secretary of the 1100 Club and my son the Editor of the 1100 Club magazine *Idle Chatter*, hence our meeting). I have three of your books but not that one.

My father bought a 1953 Jowett Bradford van, registration PNK 836, in 1960 for about £90 from a fireman stationed somewhere near Marylebone. I think it was advertised in the *Exchange and Mart*. It was his first vehicle. Having passed his test on his 17th birthday in 1937 he had never afforded a vehicle before and by 1960 was still a junior civil servant with a wife and four children so money was fairly tight. His father was a businessman and quite generous to his only child which is what kept the family going and he subsequently provided no less than four Bedford CA vans over the following years free of charge!

My father was quite mechanically minded even though he was a pen pusher and soon set to work improving the Bradford in a number of ways. He fitted Cords oil control piston rings as he thought the oil consumption was rather too high, but I seem to remember they were a disappointment as the oil consumption did not change much. He found lifting out the cylinder heads too heavy for him and rigged up some form of hoist made of ropes suspended from the garage roof trusses. He measured up for side windows (the van having no side windows at all) and larger rear ones and ordered the glass from a local supplier. He got me involved at 14 years old in fitting these windows—sanding down the edges of the holes he cut in the aluminium side panels (and steel? rear ones) and covering the edges with the old-fashioned cloth-based insulation tape prior to fitting the rubber window surrounds and then carefully inserting the new window glass with the edges lubricated with soap or similar. Many years later when helping to clear out his loft after his death I found the original rear oval glass windows and they presumably went to the council tip.

He fitted rear flashing indicators, having obtained a pair of Bedford CA rubber surrounds which needed a fair amount of re-shaping to fit the Bradford's rear curves. He had trouble with wiring them up, as after fitting a flasher unit he could not find a way to stop the trafficators going up and down in unison with the rear flashers! He approached *Car Mechanics* magazine who supplied him with a wiring diagram which enabled him to correct the problem. He also made a rear seat and seatback from wood boards and Dunlopillo, covered in Rexine and placed across the rear wheel arches I suppose, which my three younger siblings sat on (no seatbelts in those days!) while I usually occupied a sideways seat behind the driver which was actually formed from a toolbox with an opening lid (not sure if this was a Jowett fitment or had been added by the previous owner) with a cushion on it but it gave me a good view of the road ahead over my father's shoulder even if I often ended up with a stiff neck!

Coming back from a holiday on the Isle of Wight with all the family present plus two week's holiday luggage an emergency stop had to be made on the A4 in Slough for some reason which resulted in a clonk from underneath which on inspection appeared to be the rod to the rear brakes having broken free from one of its threaded couplings. The rest of the journey home was taken with some caution with the rod swinging about when taking corners!

The van was sold about two years later, I can't remember how much for, again by courtesy of *Exchange and Mart* following the arrival of the first Bedford CA and was bought by a gentleman from somewhere in South-East London. He was obviously a Bradford enthusiast as he was brought over to view it by a friend driving another Bradford.

Graham Wilkins,
Hampton, Middlesex

The Wilkins family Bradford van registered PNK 836 in c. 1960 in its original form. (*G. Wilkins*)

PNK 836 after it had been converted into a utility by the Wilkins family with windows in the sides and large rear windows. (*G. Wilkins*)

There was a short letter published in the *Daily Express* of 18 January 2018 commenting on the bad weather we were having at the time, under the heading—'Give Snow the Hard-Shoulder and Just Get on with It!' From a gentleman called Peter Hyde of Driffield, East Yorkshire, which read:

A few inches of snow and the road system falls apart (80 mph gales alert after Storm Fiona batters Britain, January 17th). How do countries who have lots of snow cope in winter? This country closes schools, shuts motorways and comes to a standstill. Is it a case of modern traffic being too flimsy to take on our rarely seen winter weather?

In the 1950s and 1960s, when deep snow covered our roads, I travelled to collect supplies in a Bradford Jowett van fitted with Town & Country tyres and didn't have a problem. They don't make them like that anymore!

Well clearly, this was a man with a story to tell, so I set about contacting him, this was not difficult as there were only two P Hyde's in the phone book, and I rang the first one, and it was the right person. It turned out that the East Yorkshire Police had five or six Bradfords all at the same time. Peter was in the Dog Section, and this was his letter to me:

In 1953 the East Riding Police started its own Dog Section after some years of relying on Railway Police Dogs. They purchased five or six Bradford Jowett vans. There was one each at Hessle, Beverley Town, Bridlington, Scenes of Crimes, Beverley and the Dog Section plus a spare (I think). I joined the Dog Section in 1957 and although I could drive I had to take the police test and did much of my training in the Bradford Jowett van. At that time, we covered the whole of the old East Riding from Norton to Withernsea and from Filey to Howden. There were two of us, P.C. Cliff Beacock handled a Dobermann named Pluto and I had a black German Shepherd called Quanta, they both were bred for police work by Surrey Police. We had to have someone on call 24/7, 365 days a year. I believe the Bradford vans would all have a running series of registration numbers but can't be certain, ours was LWF 407.

Incidentally the Chief Inspector had a Jowett Javelin, but he left the post at the same time as I joined the section and moved onto Traffic.

We used to do tracking training at a disused aerodrome at Catfoss and when they Americans arrived with the Thor missiles the officers all had huge American cars and when they saw the size of the little two-cylinder engine they couldn't believe that it was so efficient.

The only problem we ever had with the van was a broken half shaft caused when I tried to go down a cart track and got stuck. I remember one very snowy day dawned and since we were going to Beverley for dog meat, which we got from a fellmonger, the local shopkeeper asked if we could collect a couple of trays of bread as the delivery had failed due to the weather. We agreed and did so, sticking the trays on the shelf above the dog cages. The van was always smelly due to the dogs breaking wind after eating raw meat. We were rewarded with a loaf each. I did not tell my wife where the bread had travelled home. The old van seemed to be able to go anywhere with its town and country tyres and being light it rode over the top of snow.

To have a mishap in a police vehicle meant trouble with the garage sergeant. Of course, we got all over the place in all sorts of terrain, so scratches and scrapes were quite frequent. Luckily, we had a good pal who had a garage in the village and he would sort any scrapes or scratches out for free. I made use of him a couple of times.

One of the perks of the job was attending Police Dog Trials and we attended them at Otley, Durham, Middlesbrough and I went to Brighton. Because the seat in the van was, as you well know, basic we swapped it for a car seat acquired from an auto wrecker. It took me over twelve hours to get there as I had to keep stopping to give the dog a break and drink of water. There was no M25, so I went straight through the centre of London, a very tiring trip and the same journey back to face at the end of the trials which we did not do too well. I got a new dog and travelled to Preston in Lancashire to pick him up, another long trip. Yet another run was to Durham on a dog course. The van just seemed to keep going but of course it was well serviced, and we went to the force garage every thousand miles.

I recall, having been to a party the evening before, being called out to the pub at Leavening that had had a visit from a burglar. My mate drove the van because I felt a bit rough but when I got my dog out to check for tracks he led me straight to the criminal's house. The local bobby wouldn't have it and wouldn't knock on his door. The next day the man himself rang the local P.C. to give himself up as he had seen the dog on his doorstep through his bedroom window and expected a visit from the police. I had a hair of the dog and slept well when I eventually got to bed.

Eventually my colleague wrote the van off during icy weather when he crashed into a ditch. So that was the end of Bradford Jowett story.

I left the Dog Section in 1964 simply because I wanted to pass my promotion exam and get promoted.

I figure that you can pick the meat from the bones as you wish. Feel free to use any or all of it.

Regards, Peter

Bradford stories—Roger Needham

A friend of mine in my home village is a classic car fan and we meet regularly, he told me of his family's involvement with a Bradford.

My parents inherited our Bradford van in 1956. It came from 'uncle' Stan Kraus, a close friend of my Grandfather, and was used commercially at Stan's carpet shop in Nottingham. Painted dark green with black wings, the deluxe Bradford had a passenger seat and side windows. My father fitted an old bus seat in the back for the three children. The dog rode shotgun at the rear, usually.

There was an issue with the transmission. My father spent some time underneath with rather a lot of parts on the ground beside him—I suppose he replaced the clutch.

Travelling fully laden one Saturday en route to my grandparents we were stopped by a police patrolman on account of failing to display a valid tax disc. The burly figure of the officer of the law at the driver's side window terrified us all, but fortunately my father recollected that he had taxed the van, thereby avoiding being taken away to prison, by producing the new disc from his wallet.

On the way home from grandparents, the van would be even more fully laden that on the outward leg, with garden produce and grandparent goodies.

Father would take back roads over the Wolds, in order to let the dog out for a run. She would run alongside on the wide grass verge as the Bradford progressed along slowly, for maybe half a mile. I think my father himself had taken advantage of a hedge to relieve himself when we stopped, and then we set off through the dark countryside for home.

After about five minutes my Mother became agitated, wanting to know where the dog had got to—certainly she wasn't on her usual perch in the back, and she wasn't at our feet under the bus seat.

Father turned around to retrace our route and picked out in the headlight beams were two dog's-eyes, shining in the dark as the poor abandoned animal chased along trying to catch up—an emotional reunion.

The journeys in the Bradford were reliably accomplished. I suppose father would choose appropriate routes to skirt round long steep hills, but all the same, on one famous occasion he announced to us all that flat out fully laden we were doing 55 mph.

It was deemed socially appropriate as father gained promotion at work that we should ride in a car, rather than a Utility, so we upgraded to an A50. The Bradford went to my Grandmother, who painted it glossy maroon, and ran it until the early 60s when she bought a new Ford 100E van, in primer, to avoid purchase tax.

4

PERIOD ROAD TESTS

The Motor 29 January 1947
The Jowett Bradford—**£54 3**s **4**d Per Seat
 Some information about the two-cylinder Bradford Utility and the type of motoring which it provides

The ordinary motorcar is road tested by this journal at regular intervals and thus provides a comprehensive amount of data and information for the prospective owner and other interested persons. The comparatively elaborate dissection which forms the backbone of these tests is very necessary if a true picture of the unceasing development work carried out by various manufacturers is to be shown. Nor is there any less interest in such essential figures as the maximum speed and acceleration of a small family car than in the case of the 100 mph super-sports machine.

In the case of the Bradford Utility car now under review, it was, however, felt that no useful purpose could be served by investigating the performance as timed by the stop-watch and checked by a meter. This exception to the rule is justified on the grounds that the Bradford provides a basic and purely functional form of passenger or goods transport, and, as such is, in many respects, unlike anything else offered at the present moment.

It is obvious that the more a man pays for his vehicle the more he is entitled to expect, and on a form of assessment by which the number of seats available is divided into the price of the car, the Bradford scores heavily with the figure of £54 3s 4d per seat.

There is no mystery about the origin of the Bradford. It is, in fact, built by the Jowett Company and is similar in many respects to the twin-cylinder vehicles manufactured in Yorkshire for very many years. The water-cooled horizontally opposed twin was introduced by the Jowett concern in 1906, so that 40-years of development work on this power unit has somewhat naturally been turned to good account. Nor is there anything unorthodox about the suspension, transmission or steering, and one might either say that the car had been developed to such an extent where further progress is impracticable, or that, within its functional merits, an extremely satisfactory finality had been achieved.

In order to form our own opinion, the Bradford was driven for several days in conditions which alternated between heavy snow in the country and dense London traffic in fine weather. The body contains six seats, all of which have good leg-room and all-round visibility. These seats are almost instantly detachable, and a very large amount of luggage space can be made available when this was done. The seats themselves are somewhat austere, but perfectly comfortable for non-stop journeys of up to two hours' duration. The engine has all the characteristics of a robust horizontally opposed twin, except that the power output is unexpectedly smooth at anything over 20 mph in top gear, and bowling along the open road there is little or no suggestion that only two cylinders are employed. The slogging power of this engine is traditional, and in fact, is one of the most satisfactory things about the whole vehicle. There is a kind of tenacity which enables long, steep climbs to be made without the necessity of changing down, and, alternatively, the degree of acceleration and the general power made available by intelligent use of the three-speed gearbox is a further factor which does this car much credit.

Perhaps the most surprising feature of the whole chassis is the steering which is very light and requires rather less than two turns of the wheel from lock to lock, in spite of an exceptional turning circle of 34 feet. It is in fact, a form of steering which would do credit to a full-scale sporting car.

The degree of austerity precludes any attempt at sound or vibration damping, and there is undeniably a good deal of mechanical sound noticeable from the driving seat, but this is a purely functional machine which carries six people at between 40–50 mph on a petrol consumption considerably better than 30 miles to the gallon, and this remarkable economy also provides reasonable excuse for the fact that the petrol tank only holds 5½ gallons.

The Bradford Utility has the advantage that it is exempt from Purchase Tax. Its role is clearly to act as a second car for the fortunate, or as bulk family transportation to the impecunious. In either case, by its rugged construction and fine tradition of great mileages without undue wear or mechanical failure, it is likely to give utmost satisfaction.

Bradford—Essential Information Bore 79.4 mm, Stroke 101.6 mm, Swept Volume 1,005 cc, Weight 14 cwt, Power Output 19 bhp at 3,500 rpm, Wheelbase 7 feet 6 inches, Track 4 feet and half an inch, Gearbox 3-speed and reverse. Ratios—Top 4.89 to 1, 2nd 9.3 to 1, 1st 18.1 to 1, Reverse 24.7 to 1. Turning Circle 34 feet, Ignition—coil 6-volt battery, Petrol Tank Capacity 5½ gallons, Tyres 5.00 × 16 inches, Ground Clearance 7½ inches.

Weekend with a Bradford... *Motor Sport* July 1948

The Bradford product of Jowett Cars Ltd is really no mystery, for these sturdy vehicles are to be seen in increasing numbers on British roads, they are encountered on the Continent, and are now bringing home the dollars, as America has come to appreciate how handy they are as a cheeky "second-string" to bigger and faster cars.

During the Shelsley/Prescott week-end in June we covered nearly 500 miles in a Deluxe Utility version of the Bradford and the more and the harder we drove it the more it appealed to us. It would seem "just the job" for carrying the inevitable ancillaries of the racing car, for the convenience of racing motor cycles, for solving business-transport problems, as tender for the sports car, or as the sole garage-occupant of persons whose occupations, families or taste in female companionship preclude fold-flat screens and the like.

Before Mr. Baldwin placed us in a Deluxe Utility Bradford and waved us away from Jowett's Albemarle Street showrooms we rather felt that "any kind of van" would answer most, if not all, foregoing requirements. Now, after a week-end devoted, between reporting two sprint meetings, to pressing hard on the Bradford's throttle in traffic, on open road, and down by-ways and country lanes, we know, to use an Irishism, that this car is not a van.

Apart altogether from the fact that the Deluxe Utility version is properly finished within and equipped with four really comfortable leather-upholstered seats, the handling, performance and economy are all in the private-car class. In addition, this Bradford has other qualities. You sit high, with grand driver-visibility, you can pack so much into the useful body, and there is the additional charm of having something under the bonnet that is distinctly different from the dully-conventional four-cylinder engine. We cherish the unconventional and naturally enthused over the Bradford's power-unit, which is neatly summed up by a statement in the servicing data: "Firing order 1.2." From which it is abundantly apparent that here you have a modernised version of the famous horizontally-opposed two-cylinder engine which Jowetts have been making successfully since 1906.

What, you may ask, are the misdemeanours of a flat-twin, made to take its place in a vehicle of the present day? We discovered only two—in pushing on too much throttle at low engine speeds the carburettor coughed politely once or twice during the test, as if to draw attention to our clotulence, and on very isolated occasions, having eased up momentarily, we noticed a "clonk" as the flat-twin vented its confusion on the transmission. We are assured that no harm results from this occasional difference of opinion between transmission urged by the back wheels to keep going and an engine hoping for a respite. The engine starts with rather a bang, but did so every time, given choke, even after nights in the dewy open.

In other ways, this flat-twin is equal, indeed superior, to the fours. At normal and greater gaits, it is not only inaudible, but is astonishingly smooth. Rubber mounting is no doubt the answer to such sweet running, but if it is, the gearlever does not wave about like a lily in a field to proclaim it, as on many multi-cylinder cars. Actually, the engine is happy down to

15 mph in top gear. In spite of such unreasonable behaviour, this sturdy 8 hp unit, which the engineers at Idle have persuaded to develop 19 bhp at 3,500 rpm from 1,005 cc, endows the Bradford with unexpected liveliness. The 80 mph speedometer will show 50 plus along any main road for as long as you like and 60 or more comes up quite easily. In this country, of course, you have either to throw away the body or find a private road before you can do such speeds, which is a pity, because the Bradford's engine is smooth and quiet at 50 as it is at 40 or the legal 30. It is high time authorities abolished this stupidity, thus encouraging drivers more attention to what is ahead and less to what is behind. The Bradford's centre mirror is quite good but could be better still were vision not affected by vibration and the rear door pillars.

The Bradford's acceleration is as surprising as its speed capabilities, 35 mph can be had in second gear of the 3-speed box, but above 20 mph pick-up is very good in the highest ratio. Normally, therefore, you change into second as soon as you move off, then go into top at 20–25 and you still get on very nicely indeed. The engine is, obviously, well up to do its job and you will find yourself regarding it, as we did, as at least a "ten" until you check the economy of its fuel consumption.

The characteristic chug-chug exhaust note is apparent only if you put your head out of the window or stand beside the car while it ticks over, when it certainly recalls the achievement of J. J. Hall's record-breaking Jowett (54.86 mph on 7 hp for 12 hours, as long ago as 1928). In its present guise a 30 mm Zenith V-type downdraught carburettor feeds via long, water-heated induction pipes that also convey water from the engine to the radiator in its imposing chromium shell. The dynamo and battery of the 6-volt Lucas electrical system are very accessible, ignition timing and water flow are varied automatically, fuel feed is by A.C. pump, and the box-like crankcase and sump are of light-alloy. The compression ratio is 5.4 to 1 but, on "Gaitskell-white," pinking only occurred if too much throttle was given on too high a ratio up too steep a gradient.

The aforementioned briskness of the Bradford is matched by good handling qualities. True, on straight roads in a cross wind the car wandered a bit, but whether a larger rudder or more air in the tyres was the requirement we did not ascertain. We did discover that winding lanes could be negotiated in a fashion not in the least becoming to a "van" and from this ability real driver-joy resulted. The large diameter steering wheel transmits no return motion, suffers no column movement and is unassisted by castor action, while 1½ turns takes it from one moderate lock to the other. The front wheels might be non-existent. If not entirely accurate this is very reasonable steering with a tendency to oversteer and heavy at low speeds, but light enough when underway. Some lost motion was evident after 7,500 miles use.

The Girling brakes, too, were admirable—more positive as pedal pressure increased, and truly powerful without protest, effort or deviation from the required direction, unless a real crash stop was made, when they pulled to the left, but were otherwise impeccable.

These combined qualities of briskness, good handling, powerful brakes and an absence of effort from both engine and chassis make the Bradford a useful vehicle in which to hurry from A to B and on to C.

The body, apart from its car-like interior, has four windows on each side and one in each rear door. The windows in the front doors slide up and down; those immediately behind the doors open also. The rear doors are held by a single turn of the handle and the front doors and bonnet open easily. The roof light is useful, the facia lighting sensibly subdued, and the headlamps were good, but were in need of adjustment. Dipper, horn (which has a nice note) and non-cancelling direction indicator controls are accessible on an extension below the steering wheel. The central gear and brake levers are easy to reach for all save the very rheumatic, and the handbrake holds on the steepest hills, its ratchet also releasing satisfactorily.

The clutch is rather heavy and a trifle fierce, but obviously doesn't know the measuring of slip. The gearbox has constant-mesh second speed gears engaged by dog-clutches but otherwise possesses no aids-to-learners. The lever is a bit stiff to move but double-declutch changes go through well, the right-hand roller accelerator being close enough to the brake pedal to permit "heal-and-toe" action. The second-to-top change is slow and apt to be audible if hurried and sometimes obstinate if left too late. The gears are quiet, second thus being useful in traffic, and the over-run so smooth as to suggest free-wheeling, although some noise is developed. Fumes and heat are absent. The Luvac-damped ½ elliptic suspension allows considerable movement at low speeds over bad surfaces but evens out well at cruising speed. The facia has a useful cubby hole and the usual instruments, including petrol gauge, 80 mph speedometer with mileage recorder, and an oil gauge calibrated in "idle" and "driving" sections, the later indicating over 40 lb/sq. inch throughout the test. The doors lock, but a turn-switch sensibly replaces an ignition key—so easily mislaid. Electric screen wipers are provided, but the blades were rather half-hearted. The screen does not open. The choke will stay fully out if its control is turned as well as pulled out, a useful feature. The spare wheel is in a concealed tray behind the number plate and the rear pair of seats are easily removable, when 78 cubic feet of loading space becomes available. The seat backs fold for ease of entry and steps are provided. A useful tool locker is located forward of the off-side rear wheel arch. The steering wheel obstructed easy reference to the speedometer. Visibility is a strong feature of the Utility body, although the near side front mudguard is just out of sight. The fuel filler, on the mid near side, is rather small and fine threaded.

We were in a hurry nearly all the time we had the Bradford, yet it called for no oil, although a fair quantity of water was added at the end of the warm weekend. We made several climbs up a back lane to the Rising Sun Hotel at Cleeve Hill, which called for bottom gear and made the engine smell hot, but no boiling was evident. The petrol consumption, checked over the entire distance, came out at over 32 mph. No new rattles developed and those present concerned the rear doors, nor was any trouble experienced, save for a faulty bulb in one direction indicator.

Besides the Deluxe Utility which costs £415, there are available the six-seater Utility at £340, a van at £310, a lorry at £300, and a chassis at £250, inclusive of purchase tax where it applies. The impoverished post-war world so badly needs staunch transport of the sort which Idle is making that a chassis might be difficult to come by. Otherwise we would be tempted to suggest that with twin carburettors, low bonnet-line and open body, and perhaps a 4-speed Jowett gearbox and lowered chassis, the Bradford could proclaim itself an excellent austerity semi-sporting car. We would not express such an opinion had the Bradford Utility not impressed us as a very sound and pleasant vehicle during our weekend's acquaintance with it.

Engine: Two cylinders, 79.4 × 101.6 mm. (1,005 cc) RAC 8 hp, at 3,500 rpm.

Gear Ratios: 1st 18.1 to 1, 2nd 9.3 to 1, Top: 4.89 to 1, Reverse 24.7 to 1.

Tyres: 5.00 by 16 on easy-clean wheels.

Weight: 15 cwt 3 qt (in road trim with approx. 1 gallon of petrol, but less occupants).

Steering Ratios: 1½ turns lock to lock.

Fuel Capacity: 5½ gallons (range approx. 175 miles).

Wheelbase: 7 feet 6 inches. Track 4 feet & ½ an inch.

Overall dimensions: 12 feet by five feet by 5 feet 9 inches.

Makers: Jowett Cars Ltd. Idle, Bradford, and 48 Albemarle Street, London W1

Commercial Motor 3 September 1948
Australian Tour Yields Good Results

Large orders for Bradford commercial vehicles have resulted from a recent visit to Australia by Mr. T. E. Gascoyne, who has temporarily left his post as Northern sales manager of Jowett Cars, Ltd., in this country, to make a world tour. Mr. Gascoyne is now in New Zealand, and he will visit the United States and Canada before returning to Britain in December. Many of the Bradford vehicles exported to Australia and New Zealand are being sent in sections for assembly there.

13,000 Miles of Endurance—From Yorkshire to South Africa
The summer 1949 issue of *Transportation*—a Goodyear Publicity Publication

The story of how a set of Goodyear 5.50 × 16 All Weather Standard tyres brought an eight horse-power utility wagon 13,000 miles from Britain to South Africa, the trip covering every extreme of climate from icy winter in Europe to blistering heat in the Sahara Desert, is rather in the nature of an epic. Certainly, it is well worth recording, for during the trip only three tyre casualties were two punctures, caused in both cases by nails.

Co-drivers of the vehicle, a Jowett Bradford Utility, were Mr. Ronald Maxwell of Johannesburg, and Mr. John Burnaby of the B.B.C. London. There was no doubt that both drivers and vehicle put up an excellent performance in getting to South Africa on a journey that a lot of people have tried, but many have failed.

"At the end of the journey," Mr. Maxwell told a Goodyear representative in South Africa, "the tyres still had sufficient tread for many thousands of miles, despite the fact that they had travelled over rock and sand and had encountered the worst that Africa had to offer." After the cold of Europe, the Bradford Utility and its Goodyear tyre equipment had a really gruelling experience on the journey from Laghouat to Ghardaia, in North Africa. The road surface was a dour, grey stone with such a pronounced wave that speed was brought down to fifteen miles an hour in second gear. The two travellers had been advised that the best method of dealing with this would be to rush the corrugations at forty to fifty miles an hour, but the vibration when trying to reach this speed was so intense that the vehicle was compelled to crawl, while on each side of the road, monotonous rocks stretched as far as the eye could see.

After leaving Ghardaia they encountered more road corrugations, and in addition they had their first experience of a "cassis." A cassis is a dried-up water channel, crossing the road and covered in soft sand, and when the first one was encountered, and the Bradford was stuck for a time. Later it was discovered that the driving technique to employ was to rush the soft sand patches in second gear and to make a quick change down as the car began to slow up.

In the Sahara they ran into soft sand plains, 15 to 20 miles in length, and with a surface of sand finer than the grains of sugar. The only way of negotiating these plains was to rush through in second gear.

The difficulty at this stage of the journey was the amount of sand getting into the carburettor. Even with an air filter, the carburettor jets had to be cleared frequently, and because of the severe jolting the car was receiving, a broken petrol pipe which had to be re-soldered on the spot.

"But there were times in this soft sand area—which extended over 500 miles—when we had no option but to allow ourselves to be bogged down in the sand to give the engine a chance to cool," said Mr. Maxwell. The technique for getting the car on the move again was, "simple and arduous." Sand mats, consisting of an oil drum cut in half and flattened out, were placed in front of the rear wheels, and with a push from behind with the engine running, the vehicle moved over the mats to sink again in the sand on the other side. The process was repeated as necessary until a harder patch of sand was reached. On one occasion it was necessary to sand mat for an hour before the surface became firm again.

Later in the journey across the Sahara the soft sand plains became almost impassable, and the only way of negotiating was to start at 3.30 each morning, when the sand was cold and hard, to drive as fast as possible before 9 o'clock. By that time the sun began to affect the sand, and from then onwards progress was slowed down for the rest of the day.

After reaching Agades, the sand plains ended and in their place was a rocky, pitted track that abounded in concealed holes, while in Nigeria one stretch of road was so bad that it took the travellers two days to cover the 335 miles. French Equatorial Africa, roads were even worse, so much worse that at one spot both the front springs broke. The journey had to be continued to the next settlement with the weight of the body resting on the chassis.

In French Equatorial Africa and this portion of the Congo the road proved to be virtually a series of switchbacks. Unfortunately, it was not possible to travel at speed on the down sections, for at the bottom of each hill a river is found. We crossed these primitive wooden bridges with two planks to take the wheels of cars. "Once," said Mr. Maxwell, "we tried tackling a bridge at speed, but the car nearly ran off the planks into the water."

After encountering what was later discovered to be the wettest season for tropical Africa in twenty-five years, the rest of the journey, even though more bad roads were encountered (especially in Tanganyika), proved more comfortable for Mr. Maxwell and Mr. Burnaby).

On the Great North Road to Northern Rhodesia, however, they had an accident which might have led to serious consequences. Going around a corner, the rear nearside wheel flew off, but luckily for the travellers the mudguard held it in position and the car came to a stop leaning over at an angle. Upon inspection it was found that all the bolts had been stripped off the half-shaft. "The fault was ours," said Mr. Maxwell, for at a previous stop the car had been jacked up to adjust the brakes, and through our oversight this wheel had been put on again with the nuts only finger tight." Luckily, they carried a spare half-shaft with them, and worked until midnight by the roadside to get the car ready again.

"Looking back on the trip," as Mr. Maxwell wrote in an article recently published in *Mileposts* (to which magazine *Transportation* makes grateful acknowledgement for many of the details included in this article), "one salient fact emerges. The performance of the eight horse-power two-cylinder engine was a triumph for the Jowett Company, and a tribute to the high standard set by the British motor industry. The journey was undertaken in a standard model, yet the vehicle stood up to the worst that Africa had to offer. For many years there has been a prejudice against the lower-powered British car, this journey proved that an eight-horse power vehicle can travel anywhere in the world—and get there!

Intense cold, hot sand and soft sand, rocky roads and swirling quagmires and many other travelling hazards were encountered along the 13,000-mile route taken by this Jowett Bradford—a journey in which Goodyear feels honoured to have played its own essential part.

Commercial Motor 8 July 1949

Mr. J. McGregor, export manager of Jowett Cars, Ltd., leaves this month for India and Australasia. He recently visited various Continental countries. A short time ago Mr. T. E. Gascoyne, general sales manager, toured Argentina, Brazil, Uruguay and the West Indies. and last year he travelled round the world. Mr. Harry Woodhead, managing director, was in Spain for the Barcelona Fair.

Truth, 29 October 1950 (An Australian publication)

A truly convincing exhibition of power, smooth operation and general flexibility were features of *Truth's* road test of the Bradford Deluxe station wagon. The demonstration would be sufficient to prove to any cynic that a two-cylinder, horizontally opposed engine can be endowed with the pick-up, pull and quietness of a multi-cylinder job. Without digressing into technicalities, it can be said that the engine design is based on the soundest principles of engineering, has been adopted very successfully in both the motor and motor cycle fields, and from the standpoint of power output is highly efficient. The Bradford is built to meet a great variety of requirements; it will seat four in unusual comfort, in fully folding bucket seats and still leave generous loading space for station supplies or trade goods. The seats are easily removable to provide even greater freight space. Wheelbase is 7 ft. 6 in., track 4 ft ½ in., freight space with rear seat removed 4 ft. 9½ in. × 4 ft. 6 in. and ground clearance 7½ in. No Laboring The 'Bishop' cam steering was found to be restfully light and steady. The short turning circle of 34 ft. makes the Bradford one of the easiest vehicles to handle in heavy traffic and restricted parking spaces. Wide double rear doors and low platform level facilitate the handling of goods. Very high praise must be given to engine performance. The two-cylinder unit rated at 8 hp and developing 25 bhp at 3,500 rpm is astonishingly quiet and vigorous, a notable quality being its ability to function in top under load with complete absence of 'pinking' or laboring. It is built on very robust lines and is most accessible for overhaul, both cylinder heads and blocks being easily removable. Two outstanding impressions are those of safe cruising speed and good 'Girling' braking, with a hand brake that really does its job. On safe roads one can keep up a steady 55 to 60 m.p.h. without flogging the engine, and although top gear ratio is relatively high (4.89 to 1), flexibility is of a distinguished order. In second of the three forward gears (9.25 to 1) 38 mph can be maintained easily. With an 8½ cwt load of storage batteries, as well as driver and passenger, the Bradford began the eastern climb from Roseville Bridge from 30 mph in top. Later second gear was employed, and speed varied between 27 and 30 mph, finishing in that gear at 28 mph. From a 30 mph start in top, Alfred St., North Sydney, was climbed in that gear and in second, with finish at 27mph. The model, which has a normal petrol mileage of from 35 to 40 miles per gallon, was supplied by Bradford Vehicles Pty. Ltd. Its price is £741, including Federal sales tax. Sole NSW Distributors:– Bradford Vehicles Pty. Ltd. 134 New South Head Road Darling Point Phone FM 2045

The Bradford Utility Deluxe... *The Motor* 23 July 1952
A Vehicle of Sturdy Simplicity, Combining Spaciousness with Low Running Costs

Factually, and in no way critically, the Bradford utility car which we have been using for some time past must be described as a happy survivor from a past era. Frankly old-fashioned in

PERIOD ROAD TESTS AND ARTICLES

many respects of specification and appearance, it has very practical merits to commend it, and also a simple sort of charm which endeared the model to us, as it has endeared it to a great many owners.

In general chassis layout, the Bradford is essentially the same as the cars which its manufacturers, Jowett Cars Ltd, built for many years before the war. It has a twin-cylinder horizontally opposed engine of 8 hp rating, a straightforward transmission system, a simple channel-section chassis frame sprung on semi-elliptic leaf springs, and mechanical four-wheel brakes of ample size. There are plenty of modern details, such as a 12-volt compensated-voltage-control electrical equipment, synchro-mesh mechanism in the gearbox, a Layrub propeller shaft needing no lubrication, and Girling brakes which are efficient and easy to adjust. But, essentially the Bradford is simple, light in weight, totally unstreamlined and very cheap indeed to run and maintain. It is of considerable carrying capacity, and over a long period of years should provide transport at a very low average cost per mile—it may not please those who attach importance to having a car of slinky modern appearance standing outside their front door, but its road manners did please several members of our staff who had expected to be somewhat critical.

The six-light body fitted to the Bradford which we have been testing is what is known as the "deluxe" model, and has certain extra refinements compared to an alternative model costing £25 less and saving a further £13 17s 6d on purchase tax in Britain. Amongst the extras provided on the "deluxe" model are trafficators, dual windscreen wipers, short running boards, a rear bumper, and chromium plating on lamps and other parts which are painted on the cheaper model.

Two doors provide easy enough access to the individual front seats, one of which is adjustable fore-and-aft. Two more separate passenger seats of similar type are provided at the back of the car, comfortable and with very ample room around them, but even complete folding of the near-side front seat does not provide such easy access to the rear seats as is offered by most modern cars. Extra side doors would, however, obviously add cost and weight, as well as probably weakening the body structure.

At the back of the utility body, double doors open wide to give access to a very large amount of space for luggage or goods. The door opening being 40 inches high and 47 inches wide, allows for entry of bulky articles, and with the back seats in position the floor space behind them is 54 inches wide and 14 inches deep. If a full complement of four people is not being carried, however, one or both of the rear seats may be folded forward increasing the fore-and-aft depth of the luggage space to 32 inches, the minimum width of clear floor between the rear wheel arches being 40 inches. If the rear seats are removed completely (each is secured by two bolts only), the area of flat rubber-covered floor becomes 54 inches deep and 40 inches wide at its narrowest point, giving huge carrying capacity, a clear rectangular area of 15 square feet. As regards height, anything more than 25 inches high will stand above the seat backrest and begin to obstruct rearward vision, and there is internal height everywhere in excess of the 40-inch door height.

Much of the character of the Bradford on the road springs from a feature which is unique in this country, the horizontally-opposed twin-cylinder engine. This type of power unit has evident practical advantages, for whilst not unduly cheap to make, its components, few and sturdy, make for durability and low overhaul costs. The general standard of accessibility of the car's mechanical features is remarkably high, incidentally, despite such minor folly as location of the engine oil and the water fillers beneath opposite sides of the centre-hinged bonnet: although not complicated with a water pump or fitted with the fan which is an optional extra, the engine of the model tested kept comfortably cool when climbing long Devonshire hills.

Smoothness and silence comparable with that of a four-cylinder engine are frankly not offered by this vehicle, the flexibility-mounted engine suffering from certain vibration periods. An extremely inconspicuous tick-over was available, and the engine ran without fuss at top gear speeds between 15 and 30 mph or between 40 and 50 mph, its most annoying feature being a noisy vibration of the power unit and exhaust tail pipe at speeds of around 35 mph in top gear or 17 mph in 2nd ratio. This vibration period no doubt caused the breakage of a simple exhaust pipe support whilst the car was in our hands. The Bradford has no pretentions to high performance, and its acceleration (like the 8 hp cars) is markedly affected when a full load is being carried, but a determined driver will outstrip ordinary traffic in this vehicle as any other. The best open-road cruising speed is a genuine 45–50 mph, a higher rpm producing some vibration, but we did in fact cover many miles of open road at speeds up to 60 mph (with the aid of wind or gradient) and found no reason to dissent from the assurance in the running-in instructions that "after 1,000 miles, the vehicle can be driven fast continuously." Doubtless, the volume of noises in the Bradford are moderated by the use of a fabric roof covering and wooden flooring.

The three-speed gearbox has a form of synchro-mesh mechanism on 2nd and top ratios which is fully effective if it is not hustled, but cannot be described as silent, there being appreciable transmission noise even during top-gear running. The ratios are too widely spaced to give optimum performance in flat country, but it must be recalled that the Bradford is built amidst the hills of Yorkshire; an exploration of steep by-ways in Dorset and Devon revealed that 2nd gear (giving a useful 30–35 mph when necessary) would take the car up surprisingly steep hills at a plodding 15 mph, and that 1st gear provided an ample reserve of power for any gradient which we were able to discover.

Semi-elliptic front and rear springs are now rarely encountered on cars submitted to us for test, but the sturdy simplicity of this layout does still appeal to some motorists. Certainly, the riding of the Bradford is, by present-day standards, rather "lively" on rough roads, especially so far as the rear-seat passengers are concerned, but the Armstrong hydraulic shock absorbers effectively prevent any pitching. Generous ground clearance, adequate ranges of spring travel, and a concentration of weight on the driving wheels certainly make this a "go any-where" model.

So far as handling qualities are concerned, there are two definite virtues which substantially counteract what might otherwise have been accounted a substantial fault. The Bradford substantially tends to oversteer, especially when asked to make a sudden swerve, the recommended 4 lb per sq. inch difference between front and rear tyre pressures moderating, but not eliminating this characteristic.

The actual steering of the car is very light and quite high geared, however, with the result that familiarity soon makes a driver perfectly happy at the wheel. The turning circle is commendably small, thanks largely to the wheelbase being only 7 feet 6 inches, and a commendably high seating position encourages a driver to exploit the cars' manoeuvrability to the full when negotiating congested towns. A detail which some drivers noted with disfavour, however, is an accelerator pedal set at a height above the floor which is awkward for lady drivers with small feet.

The braking system seems to fall slightly short of present-day high standards, showing a maximum retardation of 0.72 g by Tapley decelerometer, by not checking the car quite as sharply as might occasionally be liked in heavy traffic conditions. No signs of "fade" were evident down long hills; however, the car was always checked in a perfectly straight line, and the central handbrake proved commendably powerful, whilst it should be recorded that a front-rear distribution of braking effort which locked the rear wheels prematurely during our routine form of test would be just right when a fuller load was being carried.

Never manufactured in sufficient numbers to bring the purchase price down to the other 8 hp cars, the Bradford nevertheless gives cause for thought, so nearly does it comply with the requirements as a "people's car." It will carry large and variable loads, comfortably and quickly enough for most purposes, at around 35-miles per gallon fuel consumption, wearing out neither itself nor its tyres with any rapidity and tackling steep hills or rough going slowly but very surely. It is a prompt starter from cold, is easily driven without any physical exertion, and incidentally with the leisurely beat of a long-stroke twin-cylinder engine pulling a 4.89 to 1 top gear ratio, it is a surprisingly pleasant vehicle to make quite long journeys.

Price £475 plus purchase tax £265 7s 9d equals £740 7s 9d
Unladen kerb weight 17 cwt. Fuel consumption 34.5 mpg
Maximum speed 53.4 mph, Maximum speed on 1 in 20 gradient 33 mph
Engine—Cylinders—2 horizontally opposed, Bore 79.4 mm, Stroke 101.6 mm, Cubic Capacity 1005 cc
Piston area 15.35 sq. in. Valves—side, Comparison ratio 5.4/1, Carburettor—Zenith downdraught 30VM
Ignition 12-volt coil, Sparking plugs—14 mm K.L.G., Fuel pump—A.C. mechanical, Oil filter—Full flow
Transmission—Clutch—Borg & Beck 7½". Top gear (s/m) 4.89, 2nd gear (s/m) 9.25, 1st gear 19.00
Propeller shaft—Layrub open, Final drive—Spiral bevel
Chassis—Brakes—Girling mechanical, Brake drum diameter—10 inches, Friction lining area 87½ sq. in.

Suspension front & Rear—semi-elliptic, Shock absorbers—Armstrong hydraulic, Tyres—Goodyear 5.00 × 16

Steering gear—Bishop cam and lever, Turning circle—34 feet. Turns of steering wheel, lock to lock—2

Acceleration Times (through gears) 0–30 mph—10.4 secs, 0–40 mph—21.0 secs, 0–50 mph—47.6 secs

Standing quarter mile—28.5 secs, Maximum speed 53.9 mph, Maximum speed in 2nd 37 mph, Maximum speed in 1st 19 mph

Weight—17 cwt, Fuel tank—6 gallons, Sump—4½ pints SAE 30 summer, SAE 20 winter

Gearbox—1½ pints SAE 40, Rear Axle—1 pint SAE 90 gear oil, Radiator—12 pints (2 drain taps)

Tyre pressures—front 24 lb, rear 28 lb, Battery—Lucas 12-volt

Commercial Motor 10 July 1953
New Bradford Range Tested *(The CD Range… NS)*

"The prototypes and several preproduction models of the new Bradford range of commercial vehicles have successfully passed the most gruelling tests and endurance runs over a period of many months," Mr. A, F. Jopling, chairman and managing director of Jowett Cars, Ltd., told the shareholders last Friday. "The tooling of two types in this range is already completed," he added *The Commercial Motor* has known of this development for two years, but the company will not release details.

5

OWNERS STORIES TODAY

OVER THE YEARS there have been so many characters within the Jowett Car Club who have owned Bradfords and have colourful stories to tell of them. I thought it would be rewarding to have a snap-shot of some of these owners in 2018, several of whom have owned Bradfords for over 50 years.

My 1953 CC Bradford Utility—Known as Bertie!

I bought my 1953 Bradford Utility (affectionately known as Bertie by the family) in 2001 from Barnard Castle which is about 65 miles from my home in Sleights near Whitby. The Bradford had been bought in a restored condition by the previous owner who had used it very little, in fact the last three years of ownership the only mileage recorded was the distance to the garage for its MOT! My wife and I went to look at the Bradford and fell in love with it—it is best described as an "oily rag" example as it is brush-painted, and the doors are not the best fitting in the world, but it is great fun! We agreed to buy Bertie and came back over to collect him on 1st April—with hindsight I should have known that this was not the best day to have arranged! My wife, Jane, and my son, Ben, came over with me in the modern and Ben (then aged 18) came back with me in the van whilst Jane brought up the rear.

The seller seemed very surprised and concerned as I said I would be driving it back to Whitby, as he had never taken it on a long run previously. We travelled through Barnard Castle, but as soon as we came out of the town and I took it above the 30 mph speed limit there was a terrible vibration on the steering, it was so severe I could hardly hold the steering wheel. I soon realised that if I let it come back to 30 mph, the vibration stopped.

This effectively reduced our travelling speed to 30 mph, so it was going to be a long 65 miles! This was quite frustrating, as I had to brake going down gradients to keep my speed down to 30. Anyway, we got to Darlington and then to Middlesbrough where we needed to cross the dual carriageway onto the Whitby road. Needless to say, this was the place it decided to stall so Ben and I pushed it to the side of the road, out of the way. After a bit of tinkering, it was with great relief that it started again, so we set off again for Whitby at our steady 30 mph.

We carried on towards Whitby and I managed to get about five miles through Guisborough, and seventeen miles from home. I pulled into a car park and was becoming over confidant, saying we were on the last lap, just as I was starting off again from the car park the Bradford stalled, and was very reluctant to restart. After a lot of messing about I managed to get it running again and it and was buzzing along nicely at 30 mph for several miles and I was starting to think I would have an uneventful remaining ten miles—this was a mistake! I was climbing a steep rise with double white lines down the middle of the road, as it was a blind rise. It was at this point my exhaust fell off, and was rubbing along the road, with sparks everywhere. I jumped out to assess the situation, while Ben and Jane directed traffic. The exhaust had snapped just in front of the silencer but had not broken right through. In view of the starting problems, I decided to leave the engine running and got my hacksaw out to remove the tail section. This I did, I put everything back in the rear of the van and got back into the driver's seat ready for the off. As soon as I shut the door the engine stopped and would not restart for love or money. Coast traffic was building up behind, so it was a very stressful situation that lasted for the best part of half an hour. I was just debating ringing the insurance company for breakdown assistance when I managed to start it again!

The rest of the journey was rather noisy, but uneventful, I pulled into lay-bys as often as I could to allow backed-up coast traffic past, as by this time the road was very busy. Was I pleased to see the Sleights sign? Yes, I was, but we were not finished yet! Just as I was coming up the steep hill through the village, the back doors swung open, so I came to a rapid halt outside the village hall, as I could see in my mirror that my tool box was sliding towards the open doors, I jumped out and quickly closed them again. I set off and was delighted when I reached my driveway! It only took 5 hours to do the 65-mile journey!

After this trip I soon had the wheels balanced that resolved the vibration problem at 30 mph—I can now manage 50 mph on a good day with the wind behind me. A new exhaust system was soon put together and the engine was reconditioned and has run well ever since. I did, however, have a small fire behind the dashboard a few years ago on the way to Whitby at the very busy "Four Lane Ends" roundabout on the outskirts of town. I had to push Bertie into a side street and call out the breakdown service to take me home. The lad who came was very efficient and had me on the low loader in no time. He then took is iPhone out and started to take pictures of it, I asked him if he was interested in old cars, to which he said, "Nah, but we have a competition each month to see who has picked up the most obscure vehicle and I am as sure as hell going to win it this month!"

My good friend, David Pomroy, who lives in the village, is good with electrics, replaced the two burnt-out wires and got me back on the road in no time. I have also added an electric fan off a VW Golf that fitted like a glove, as I tended to over-heat a little on the many hills in my area, this problem has now been solved. I could go on to add dozens of anecdotes such as when I wanted to fit new carpets in the van, the lad in the local carpet shop asked me what I was wanting to use the heavy-duty carpets for. When I told him that they were for my Jowett Bradford he gave me a discount and then asked if he could come and fit them for me, to which I said, "Of course!" The end result was a far better job than I could ever have done! I will have to leave other stories to another time, as there are just too many to publish here.

This was my 1953 Bradford utility registered PTE 708 when it was owned by my good friend Trevor Hartley in 1969, it changed hands several times after this. I bought it from a gentleman in Barnard Castle in 2001 and it has been on the road ever since. (*T. Hartley*)

Me with my Bradford on 'Drive it Day' in 2014. (*Jane Stokoe*)

Waiting for a train at Grosmont railway station on the North Yorkshire Moors Railway in 2012 on the way home from the vintage vehicle rally there. (*Jane Stokoe*)

Driving through the ford at Hovingham, near Castle Howard during the scenic run at the Jowett Car Club international rally based in York in May 2004. (*Jane Stokoe*)

Jowett Bradford an Autobiographical statement by Paul Beaumont

"Jowetts don't die, they are left to the next of kin" so ran one of the prosaic Jowett adverts of the 1930s. In my case it was somewhat the other way around—I was born into them—almost born in one!

By way of explanation, my parents spent the Second World War years working for the Civil Service in East Anglia. When peace returned my father decided that he had had enough of that life and when he and my mother married in 1950 he decided to purchase a small holding in rural Northamptonshire. Up to this point, dad's mode of transport had been a bicycle—albeit a top of the range bicycle. Realisation quickly dawned that a mechanically propelled vehicle was going to be needed for this new life. A family apocryphal tale says that dad enlisted the services and advice of a friend to decide between a CB model Jowett Bradford van and an Austin A40 pick-up. The friend advised in favour of the Jowett (his name was Hargreaves and he hailed from Rochdale so maybe he was biased!) and the low mileage, ex-fishmonger's HER 726 became only the second vehicle in the small hamlet that was to be mum's home for the next 66 years. This was probably a fortuitous choice as by 1958 our family numbered 7!

I made an appearance in 1953, my pregnant mother being conveyed to the maternity hospital in Banbury and home again with me a few days later in HER 726. So, began my Jowett association!

In recent years my mother would explain my Jowett fascination by explaining that when I was an infant the Bradford would be reversed onto the smallholding with me asleep in a carrycot in the back, so I could be watched whilst essential jobs like hoeing lettuces, picking peas and beans or pruning fruit bushes were undertaken.

The smallholding provided a reasonable living during the spring to autumn period, but the winter months were lean, so dad bought (or maybe was given!) a small rural milk round which in its 20-mile daily tour managed to include 3 counties! It also meant that the Jowett had to work 7 days a week and 364 days a year—Christmas day usually being serviced on Christmas Eve, probably by overloading the poor Jowett.

The Bradford was serviced by Jowett agents Banbury General Motor Company which stood (now long demolished) on the corner of North Bar and Warwick Road, almost opposite the police station. However, servicing costs and the time constraint—there was no money for vehicle hire!—eventually led to Dad deciding to do it himself. This inevitably meant that HER joined a huge number of small vans in the hands of similar businesses that were over worked and poorly serviced.

In 1956 disaster struck. With my mother on enforced bed rest as she was unwell whilst expecting my twin sisters my younger brother and I were accompanying Dad on the milk round. We were parked at the side of the A43 in the days before the needs of Silverstone demanded its conversion to a dual carriageway, when an inebriated "lady" driver ran into the rear of the Bradford which was full of milk bottles. My 2-year old brother was rescued from the debris, totally unscathed whereas I sustained a cut to my head that has rendered me a small bald patch throughout my life! HER was rebuilt by the insurance company and returned to service.

HER was the family transport as well as a business vehicle. One of its duties was the school run. One morning when carrying out this task a half shaft failed just behind the rear wheel. The vehicle came to a halt supported partly by the wheel in the rear wheel arch and partly by the brake drum! A call to Banbury General Motor Company ensued and a replacement shaft arrived that evening courtesy of British Rail, from Howden Clough. HER was back on duty the following day!

In the late 1950s Bradfords were not uncommon on the roads of South Northamptonshire. As well as ours, the local grocer also ran a CC model which, by 1960 was beginning to look untidy. One day the grocer approached my father with a view to selling it to him. The deal was done and twelve pounds ten bob! changed hands. The body of this van (RFC 326) was in very poor condition so dad spent a winter exercising his carpentry skills rebuilding its rear with quite exceptional results. Before this could be completed however, HER decided, one Sunday morning, to evict the off-side con-rod through the crankcase causing major devastation to the engine. A quick examination showed that RFC's engine was totally different to that of HER and therefore not a viable exchange unit (today I know that exchanging the engine and gearbox, together with some chassis cross members could have resolved this!) HER was

BRADFORD OWNERSHIP TODAY

abandoned and eventually time and weather took its toll and it collapsed. Today I own it and it is slowly being restored, being used each year at the Practical Classics Restoration Show, as a working exhibit.

Dad progressed work on RFC as quickly as he could, working mainly in the open during the short days of the 1960–61 winter and it was in service before Easter.

Day by day RFC valiantly trudged the daily 20 miles or so, including every day of the horrific winter of 1962/3. On the day that the last of the snow disappeared disaster struck. RFC broke its crankshaft. It was recovered to a small garage in Brackley where a friend of dad's worked. Dad was loaned (presumably with the eye on a sale) a fairly tired Jowett Bradford Utility Deluxe. Dad rang Bert or Fred or George, I do not recall his name, who was foreman at Banbury General Motor Company, who surprisingly said that they had a spare CC engine, but it was in the air raid shelter. They would need a couple of days to dig it out! I went with Dad to collect it. When we arrived, there was a vehicle there that I did not recognise (I had always had an interest in cars and in the pre-import saturation era, could recognise most models) This turned out to be a CD Bradford making what must have been one of its last deliveries from Howden Clough.

"New" engine installed RFC resumed duties. By now I was in secondary school and I realised that the Bradford's engine was different to most motor cars and this fascinated me. The 1960s after Howden Clough closed were a difficult time to maintain a Bradford especially one that was required to be available daily. Throughout my secondary school years, I regularly assisted maintaining the Bradford, very much on a make do and mend principle. On one occasion *Exchange and Mart* carried an advert for a load of Bradford spares in Rickmansworth. Dad decided to buy these and we borrowed a friend's Standard Atlas van to collect them. Now the Bradford does not enjoy lively performance, but an 8 hp Standard Atlas with over a ton of Jowett parts on board could be described as pedestrian at best! Nevertheless, these parts ensured that RFC managed to perform with some degree of reliability!

As I studied for my 'A' levels a malady afflicted the Bradford's gearbox leaving it with a colossal oil leak and only second and top gear, meaning that the milk round had to be achieved without the need for reversing. It also had to be punctuated with lubrication replenishment stops! Numerous second-hand gearboxes were purchased and returned—probably all belonging to a Bedford rather than a Bradford. Finally, Charlie Moar came to the rescue with a gearbox that he vouched for as being good—he had been using it until the vehicle broke a half shaft! I spent the evening before I took my 'A' level maths exam fitting it.

'A' levels over my involvement with the Bradford had excited an interest in mechanical engineering and I took an honours degree at Cardiff University and on graduation, joined Lucas Girling. With me only at home for the weekends, maintaining the Bradford was too much for Dad alone and he eventually bought an Austin A35 van followed by a succession of mini vans (most of which involved my maintenance skills—I quickly learnt that it is not possible to change a gearbox in a mini in an evening!)

I begged dad to let me have RFC. It needed substantial work and a lot of chassis repair. He refused saying that he intended putting it back on the road! This never happened.

In the late 1970s I was working for Lucas Girling in South Wales and I saw a derelict Bradford for sale in London, in *Exchange and Mart*. This had an interesting registration number, so I bought it chiefly because of the number. Like Dad's it needed substantial chassis work. I stripped it and added a couple of other derelict vehicles to my portfolio.

Family commitments and a gas explosion that destroyed our South Wales home, curtailed my activities for a few years and my father passed away in 1981. My mother told me that all of the Jowett stuff was mine, but it was difficult to extract RFC from its resting place and it remained where it was until after my mother passed away in 2016.

In the early 1980s The Jowett Car Club's Bradford registrar was Nick Coppin. I heard that Nick was looking to relieve himself of the responsibility. I decided that I would like to have a go at the job but had no idea how Jowett Car Club politics worked, so I contacted Nick. The next thing I received was a pack of cards from a card file system and a floppy disc! I was the Bradford registrar!

In 1995 I moved to Yorkshire, to take up a new job in Huddersfield and in so doing released some capital.

I decided that as registrar I really ought to have a Bradford on the road so I obtained a quotation for repairing my original Bradford chassis. £1,500! At the same time a long standing JCC member alerted me to a Bradford utility for sale in Guildford. The price: £1,500. I went to see it. The owner knew nothing about it, having taken it in part payment for a debt—all he wanted was his money back. I said we had a deal if I could see it running—we had gone equipped with fuel and a spare battery. We cleaned the points, stuck some fuel in, coupled up the battery and swung it over with the crank handle. On about the tenth pull it fired and two pulls later it ran much to the amazement of the vendor! FOU 416 was mine!

This vehicle came with its bonnet secured with gaffer tape as the hinges were broken. Removing the tape removed the paint beneath it. It also came with a board that proclaimed that it had recently been restored and been returned to its original colour—supported by attached photographs—black and white photographs!

It took me three years to get FOU to a point where I was happy to submit it for an MOT. Today it is untidy to look at but quite reliable. Recently I was able to buy GKU 954—a CC Utility deluxe that was once Jowett's own demonstrator. It is not yet reliable!

I continue to serve as Bradford registrar and am regularly apprised of new unknown vehicles, vehicles that have been scrapped and log books that are for sale, usually on eBay. That said, today the register records the details of just 422 Bradfords out of the 40,000-ish built. Of those fewer than 40 are described as roadworthy.

Bradford Ownership Today

Paul Beaumont has been the Bradford registrar for the Jowett Car Club for many years he is on the right of this picture talking to me in front of his Bradford HER 726 at the restoration show at the NEC Birmingham in March 2015.

Another view of Paul Beaumont's Bradford registered HER 726 at the restoration show at the NEC Birmingham in March 2015. It has appeared at the show each year since and now it is well on the way to a full restoration.

This Bradford registered FOU 416 is also owned by Paul Beaumont it is an early example as it has sidelights on the front wings. This picture was taken at the Jowett Car Club national rally at Castle Howard near York in May 2004.

This is the latest Bradford to join Paul Beaumont's fleet, GKU 954 was originally owned by John Baldwin who was the sales manager at the Jowett showroom at Albemarle Street, London. It was later owned by his son, Nick Baldwin, the motoring correspondent and finally bought by Paul in April 2018.

Another view of Paul Beaumont's Bradford registered GKU 954, taken at the Jowett Car Club national rally in Harrogate in May 2018.

These are the remains of Paul Beaumont's father's Bradford registered RFC 326, I wonder if this will be Paul's next project, he's a braver man than me! (*P. Beaumont*)

My Bradford FAK 464–Richard R. Rhodes

In 1951 when I was nine years old my father decided that his growing family would no longer fit into the Triumph twin bike and sidecar outfit. Larger transport was called for. It had to be a van type body because his garage was so narrow he would have to drive in and clamber out of the rear.

A friend told him of a van in Bradford, called a Jowett Bradford which was for sale. We went over to see it and duly bought it. FAK 464 was a dark blue 1948 CB Utility with 38,000 miles on the clock.

Six of us inside (two adults and four children) the Bradford on a sunny day was quite stuffy! So, my father removed the four side windows and fitted two sliding ones, which soon cured the problem.

For the next eight years we enjoyed many thousands of miles of trouble-free motoring. Apart from routine maintenance, the only jobs I recall helping with were a clutch and a rebore.

On my 17th birthday I had my first drive but could not master double de-clutching for ages. So, at every hill I had to stop and engage first! After a few lessons on a Minor 1000, I eventually took and passed my test in the Bradford. To my surprise, after the test my father handed the log book to me and said the Bradford was mine!

At the time I had a girlfriend who did not like going out on my motorbike as it blew her hair about, so when the Bradford came, she was very happy. Not many of my contemporaries owned four wheels, so this added to the bliss of unruffled hairstyles.

After a small accident I fitted motorcycle mudguards and painted her powder blue with flames on the bonnet, not to mention whitewalls! On my honeymoon in Cornwall the law stopped us for a vehicle check—they thought we were hippies! Returning from Truro to Derby took 10½ hours for the 366 miles, with the original seats—Oh the pain!

During the 1966 "Back Britain" campaign I painted a Union Jack on the bonnet. Returning from South Wales an ominous knocking heralded a broken con rod, the last fifteen miles into Derby, on one cylinder, we were overtaken by a milk float. After repairs I took a few light haulage jobs including moving fish tanks complete with fish and a 5" gauge steam loco. Whilst carrying a load of sand I came to a gentle halt, engine running and in gear. When I peered underneath the prop shaft was revolving and walking round the offside I nearly fell over the wheel which was sticking out of the axle about a foot. So, I jacked it up and pushed it back and slowly drove home. This was not too far fortunately, and on stripping it down I found that two lock nuts had loosened, allowing the half shaft to come adrift, it was soon repaired.

On one bad Derbyshire winter night my next door neighbour came home from town to inform me that I would not be able to get into work for my night-shift because of the state of the roads and the depth of the snow. I set off with confidence knowing the Bradford's sure footedness and arrived safely just five minutes later than usual.

BRADFORD OWNERSHIP TODAY

Better stopping power was called for after a nasty near miss on a steep hill in the Derbyshire Peaks. After obtaining 10" brake drums, shoes and back plates and a little drilling, they were safely fitted, resulting in much better and long-lasting brakes.

I began to realize that "Betsy" (so named by my daughter) and her kind were becoming rare animals and I'd better start looking after her. So off came the cycle wings and correct ones fitted. A new roof—the original was damaged by baboons at a safari park, and a fresh coat of chocolate and black paint.

In 1977 we took a holiday in the Isle of Wight but coming home across the island disaster struck. When the engine can be turned on the handle, but the flywheel doesn't turn, something's amiss— broken crankshaft. We pushed Betsy into a kind resident's drive, who promised to look after her. I returned the following week with a borrowed tow truck. After a long drive I got her home—why do these things always happen so far away from home? Luckily, I had a spare engine at home to put in.

I could go on and talk about Betsy, she is one of the family. After travelling in her man and boy for over 200,000 miles I feel I just about know her….

This is how the story originally ended when it appeared in our club magazine, *The Jowetteer* in April 1986, which was an issue dedicated to the Bradford. As Richard still owns Betsy, I asked him to bring the story up-to-date, which I am very pleased to say, he agreed to …

In 1986, after many years of everyday use with the Bradford, I decided to buy a second car. This allowed more extensive repairs of Betsy to be undertaken. This included replacing the roof which, as mentioned before, had been damaged by a friendly baboon at a safari park, who decided to try and break in, scaring my children half to death as they saw the baboon's fingers poking through the wadding right above their heads. I also replaced the deck timbers and floor and re-sprayed her in the original dark blue with black mudguards.

In Shardlow, the village I have lived in for nearly fifty years, Betsy is something of a landmark, although these days she spends her down time sheltering from the weather in my garage. On holiday in Bridport, in Dorset, we drove over a thousand miles in a week. My wife and I were visiting Portland Bill, enjoying our holiday, when in the car park we heard a shout of, "You're a long way from Shardlow!"

Betsy has been involved in many vintage car rallies and shows, Jowett Car Club events, village fetes, family holidays, weddings and fun rides out for young nieces, nephews and my grandson. I have heard numerous tales from strangers who tell me that they/their father, brother, grandfather or uncle used to own her. I know they cannot have all owned her, but I let them tell the story anyway.

Over the years she has had a variety of paint jobs, including flames coming up the bonnet, purple with yellow wheels, orange and navy in alternate panels, but now in her old age she is more dignified!

I first drove Betsy 57 years ago, and 320,000 miles later she drives better than ever, and still gets many admiring glances and comments.

Richard Rhodes, January 2018

Richard Rhodes with his son, Jerad, at the Jowett Car Club international rally in Tewkesbury in May 2016.

The rear view of Richard Rhodes' Bradford with a selection of period memorabilia on display.

A Bradford Ditty.... by Steven Grey

Berni, that's my name, DBW 528 is my number. I started out as a 1948 CB Bradford, still going strong I'd like to add. Out at 7.45 a.m. every morning and back at 4 p.m., hail, rain, snow or shine—reliable I have been, although a little tired I do get at MOT time. It seems they and I just don't agree, some worn parts are there to see, but how much will they allow, so that I can go on. This year it was quite painful, my right-hand side had gone quite bad, that scourge of age had attacked my chassis. Nothing for it, major surgery it had to be. A replacement part was grafted in to keep me going, the old one had done fine service, had been with me since the start.

Now I'm growing old, I'm losing track of what is original, could be I'm not the motor I started out as. The engine and body numbers agree, but they are only held on by screws you see, they could have been changed from part to part just to keep me looking smart. Cylinders, crank, axles and gear boxes have all been done.

Back in 1971 I moved from Banbury where I had begun for Brackley Saw Mills I had worked, before returning to my supplier, Banbury General Motor Company, to be used by them before being laid up. From there I was rescued, my new home was to be Wordsley, my new guardian was quite young (18), a van I was, not bad it seemed to those young eyes, sunshine roof and all, but underneath all was not good. I struggled on for a time before being laid up for a rest again. In 1975 I was resurrected to serve again, this time I had changed to a pick-up, cut off at the waist. For twelve months more I travelled on, bits of wood falling off in places that mattered quite a lot. By now it was quite plain that a rest was coming.

So, on went the covers for a while this time, it took to the spring of 1980 for enthusiasm to be rekindled (the pocket also). Concours I could never be, I'd gone too far it was plain to see. So, a compromise it was to be, quite excited I felt. The work started in earnest, all stripped down I was, not one bolt left undone. My chassis was painted and re-assembled, my engine, gearbox, axles too all refurbished and refitted. Six cubic feet of timber and many litres of paint were used to get me looking great—twelve months of constant work it had taken.

The MOT man was not happy, the brakes were not good enough he said, "cannot bed them in 'till I've got that ticket was the reply." So off he went on his trade plates, after which he was quite happy. So, there I was, a label in the window and ready to go. Perhaps he was quite lucky not to suffer from what was to follow. A severe case of the shakes on the front end. It seemed to start from nothing, a slight change in the camber at 25–30 mph, and off it would go, quite frightening as many know, especially on-coming motorists. My problem it was traced to something quite different to that of no wheel balance, bad caster or track. With me it was my guardian trying to be clever, fitting needle rollers instead of bronze bushes. The steering was light and responsive, but this was wrong you see, the damping action of those bushes is quite necessary to stop me wobbling like a jelly!

Since then I've carried beauty queens, been to rallies and generally enjoyed myself.

Give me a wave if you see me....

This is how the story originally ended when it appeared in our club magazine, *The Jowetteer* in April 1986. As Steven still owns Berni Bradford, I asked him to bring the story up-to-date, which I am very pleased to say, he agreed to....

I continued my daily routine for another couple of years until a forced change of employment for my keeper meant a different commute route, this involved a busy section which was almost always stop-start, as anyone who has driven a Bradford with the Jowett clutch arrangement will know they don't always engage smoothly, even when carefully set up, sometimes it feels like the engine wants to jump out from under the bonnet.

As the financial position allowed, a more modern vehicle was purchased, and I was allowed a more leisurely existence kept nice and cosy in a garage.

When I was taken out it was usually with a load of something to carry whether it was rubbish to the local recycling centre or tools to a job. Occasionally a leisure ride was in order.

Over the years I was only afflicted by some minor problems, a perished fuel pipe, a sticking exhaust valve, corroded inlet manifold leaking water into the cylinder and a head gasket failure, all on the same cylinder.

By now it was 2015 and the Jowett Car Club's next National Rally was going to be held around 30 miles away at Upton on Severn. It was my chance to attend, a wash and polish was in order, in addition one or two bits of paintwork needed attention.

Upon investigation the tin worm had got the better of the bottom edge of my front nearside wing, so some new metal was grafted in and suitably painted. In addition, my roof cloth had split and was also replaced. I was ready to go.

In the weeks leading up to the rally it was discovered that the bell housing had developed a crack above the starter motor, it was decided that it should make it to the rally and back before needing to be replaced.

In true Jowett style I made it there and back without any problem. When I was converted some years ago I was promised a set of wooden sides so that I could look extra special when I was not at work.

Now my owner is nearing retirement he has once again promised me that I will get them as part of a further tidying up of my bodywork especially as I have a date with some other friends from Idle in 2018.

Meanwhile I am comfortable in my garage dreaming of the open road.

Steven Grey November 2017

I am pleased to say that both Richard and Steven attended the first ever Bradford-only in their Bradfords, but more of that later!

Bradford Ownership Today

Steven Grey bought this 1948 Bradford van in 1971, registered DBW 528 when he was 18 years old, it was in a poor state and needed a rebuild, he converted it into a lorry. (*Steven Grey*)

This is the Bradford lorry conversion registered DBW 528 that Steven Grey created back in 1971 and he still owns it 47 years later! The picture was taken at the Jowett Car Club international rally in Tewksbury in May 2016.

Alan Bartlett, 1953 Bradford Lorry—*The Tramp*

Tramp was advertised in the *Classic Motor Monthly* paper in February 2014. My friend Barrie, who dabbles with classic car sales spotted it and asked if I was interested. A while later the deal was done and being arranged to transport to its new home in Somerset. It arrived with me in March. One late evening, a Jowett Bradford Lorry, with a lorry load of spares that came with it. He had spent the last almost 35 years in a garage in Northumberland. A snapped crank was told by the last owner to be the reason for this. Though over the years the previous owner had been accumulating parts for an eventual engine rebuild.

The extensive paperwork with the car is a fascinating read, all the receipts and letters for work done or enquiries for new parts and replacement bits. Along with some documents of when it was in first use as a florist's vehicle from the 50s. Barber Brothers of Forest Hall in Newcastle Upon Tyne.

Once it arrived, I had begun assessing what I had actually bought, having never really had anything to do with Bradfords before. As soon as I opened the door, you could see the door had dropped, both doors in fact. The A posts where they were attached, were past their best and had been patched together with bits of pine in the bottoms to try and prolong their life.

Many holes in the scuttle side panels, somewhere the wings were barely attached. An interesting patch of aluminium on one wing riveted, holding on the front headlight. This I have kept on adding to its character.

On further inspection, the chassis was very rotten from the rear back, poking through with a screw driver to reveal all the holes. It was also bowing outwards where the metal had been fatigued from heavy loads. A local metal fabricator made up completely new chassis rails from two C shaped pieces of steel, to form and remake the rear.

The bodywork was patchy with more holes, and pieces which had just rotted away. A friend of mine, Andy. who loves old mechanical things, and quite handy with a welder has been slowly helping me patch up and mend all the metal work, very cleverly remaking and reshaping new repair patches.

From the start I did have a thought to respraying, but later on I thought it would be nice to keep its garaged patina, still thinking on a viable covering to protect it from getting worse. It was always going to by a sympathetic renovation. To get all the mechanicals together and running nicely and keep the shabby body in a preserved condition. Patina is the word.

I started with removing the doors, which sat in the back, then out came the dashboard and old wiring. After that, I removed the front axle to strip it down to paint and renew kingpins. I cleaned up the front of the chassis, then eventually made the decision to take off the cab and bed. Before long I was down to a pair of axles and a chassis. With a pile of bits awaiting refurbishment. Two big tins of anti-rust primer, and chassis black were on their way to suitably tidy up the mechanical bits. Space has been a premium in the workshop, so the cab was sat on the bed, to save space, while given a liberal de-rusting and red oxide priming underneath while up ended.

I have outsourced some of the jobs I couldn't do, for example the chassis welding, and the woodwork. A local chap in the next town who makes bodies for BSA three wheelers was able to make up suitable new ash frame, from the old pine patterns. This was completed early last year to get the doors back on.

The engine has had new bearings throughout, sourcing another donor engine from the car club, the engine is the last milestone before I can actually say I've sat in and had a drive in the four years of ownership. I am very much looking forward to having two working Jowetts on the road. Perhaps later on in life a third open top would complete the set!

Alan has in fact just taken *The Tramp* to the Bristol Classic Car Show which was held on 16 and 17 June 2018 in its part-restored state, which created a great deal of interest with the show spectators, this will be the first show of many *The Tramp* will be attending—well done Alan!

The 1934 Jowett saloon, known as *The Lady* and Bradford lorry, known as *The Tramp*, owned by Alan Bartlett. Alan has used *The Lady* continuously for many years and has a blog on social media called *The Lady's Great British Tea Room Tour*, Alan describes himself as a blogger and cake enthusiast! (*Alan Bartlett*)

Alan Bartlett has been restoring his Bradford lorry known as *The Tramp* for some time and is now roadworthy. He intends to restore it mechanically but leave the bodywork as original as possible. (*Alan Bartlett*)

Bradford ENV 36—Alastair Gregg

As mentioned previously, the first ever rally for Bradfords only took place over the early May bank holiday 2018 in Buxton. The hotel used for our base is owned by Alastair, who has a beautiful Jowett Jupiter sports car. In late 2017 he bought the remains of a Bradford Utility which he showed me during the weekend. It is in a terrible state and completely dismantled, but I am sure he will make a great job of it. He goes on to say:

> I have only had the Bradford about a month, so changes are very limited at the moment, please find attached a number of photographs for you to chuckle at. The engine was kept separately and was bought to start work on the project some while ago. Michael Kavanagh now has it and will get it going for me. It was originally a Utility but since there is virtually nothing left I am going to try to make a lorry out of it. The project may take some while as I am aiming to brush up on my woodworking and welding skills. Moving the Bradford onto the trailer to bring it home was the first time it had moved in 27 years!
>
> Alastair Gregg, November 2017

I was literally just going to post my manuscript off to my publishers when I noticed that the October issue of *Classic & Sportscar* magazine featured Alastair's Bradford, saying:

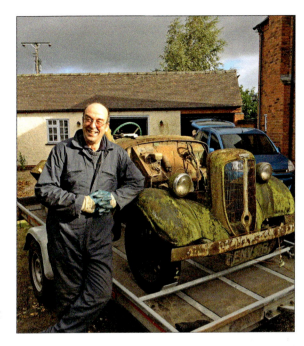

Alastair Gregg owns a lovely Jowett Jupiter sports car, in October 2017 he bought this very sad-looking Bradford utility registered ENV 36 that had been languishing in a garden for twenty-seven years. The restoration is now well underway! (*Tim Brown*)

Alastair Gregg of Buxton recently found a Jowett Bradford Utility described by fellow enthusiast, Tim Brown, as requiring 'heroic restoration'. ENV 36 was built in 1948 and registered in Northampton. In the 1960s the Utility was found bricked-up in a garage and spent the next half century stored outside before Gregg bought it in October 2017. 'There is very little bodywork' he said, 'but there are some body panels that should make some good patterns. The Jowett Car Club has some drawings of the ash frame, so I have some skills to learn'.

Bradford GET 898—Keith Wear

The truth is that by a great margin I have driven trusty Bradfords for well over 40,000 miles!

In 1951 I learned to drive on FKW 44, now owned by Morrisons, but from new it was owned by my Father's medium size but very successful textile manufacturing business. In addition to local runs, after about six months I drove the van every two weeks throughout the year from Bradford to Horwich in Lancashire. I did this for almost two years delivering a full and heavy van-load of cloth to a processor in Horwich and collecting a return load of processed material. There and back in one day the route was via Halifax, Sowerby Bridge, then climbing the winding and steep A58 over the Pennines before dropping down the long incline into Lancashire. Bearing in mind the heavy load, this section entailed dropping to second gear several times and using brakes as well on corners to reach Littleborough. There the route followed on to Rochdale, Bury, Bolton and a further 11 miles to Horwich. The company I went to was named Jolly & Jackson, but in snowy winters I can tell you there was nothing jolly about the journey!

One time, with a few inches of snow already on the ground, a heavy snowfall started as I climbed up the Pennines on the A58 from Sowerby Bridge. I pulled in thinking I had better turn back, when a snow plough passed me. Off I went close behind him. He ploughed many miles to the moor tops and stopped at the county boundary! I went down into Lancashire slower than ever with visions of setting off like a skier and going over the edge at a bend. Needless to say, I completed the job in the Bradford climbing the hills once again on the return journey. Having had a terrible day, I returned to the city of Bradford very late!

As a 'classic' I bought GET 898, (the Bradford Utility Deluxe which is now owned by Barbara Atack) and in thirteen years I went as far south as the JCC Rally at Leeds Castle in Kent and as far as one can drive north to the Northernmost point of the Shetland Islands. Of course, the Bradford attended many JCC Rallies elsewhere and other shows around the country, I attended two in Scotland.

I only had two significant breakdowns, a broken half shaft when returning from Biggar and a broken crankshaft in the Yorkshire Dales a few miles from our then home. Like you, I'm not an automobile engineer, but I have sorted out several breakdowns due to the simplicity of the vehicle and kept on going.

John & Barbara Atack—Bradford GET 898

This Bradford has to be one of the most famous Bradfords around, as it was used extensively by Keith Wear until he bought a Javelin and so John & Barbara Atack became the new custodians. Sadly, John died in February 2015, but Barbara still owns the Bradford and uses it extensively during the rally season. She took it to the first Bradford-only rally and the Jowett Car Club international rally in May 2018. There is an information board that Barbara has in the window when attending rallies, which reads as follows:

This early example of an estate car was produced by Jowett Cars, Idle, Bradford. Mechanically it reflects pre-war practices that follow early Jowett concepts going back to Edwardian times.

GET 898 was supplied in November 1951 by H. & B. Motors (Rotherham) to paint manufacturers J. P. McDougall & Co. Ltd of Manchester. In 1956 it returned from exile to West Riding ownership having five more owners until 1971. Then, GET 898 became a playground fixture at a Morley school before being confined to the indignity of a scrapyard.

In 1976 she was rescued by Eric Moore who restored her including repainting in the original ex-works colour 'Catalina Tan' that was obligatory for a Utility Deluxe. She has made

The Morrison's van was restored on their behalf in the mid-1980s, which at the time, was an expensive restoration. Their new headquarters were built on the old Jowett factory site at Five Lane Ends, Idle, Bradford. The Bradford has been used by them for publicity ever since. It also attends local country shows, such as the Great Yorkshire Show in Harrogate. It was originally owned from new by Keith Wear's father.

Another view of the Morrison's Bradford showing the period grocery display in the rear, both these pictures were taken at the Jowett Car Club international rally in Harrogate in May 2018.

various appearances on TV and in film over the years and recently featured on 'Look North' in celebration of the Jowett production centenary.

Her present custodian has inherited her from John Atack, her husband, and plans to take her to some shows each year in his memory, especially Hebden Bridge which was his home town. John drove her extensively for the past 12 years including several tours of Northern France, Spain and Denmark. In many of these years she won the J.C.C. award for the most travelled side-valve vehicle. She has motored over 10,000 miles in a two-year period and in October 2014 completed another 1,200-mile round trip to Brittany over a twelve-day tour.

GET 898 shared a home with her older friend, a 1929 Jowett Long Four Tourer which now has moved to Scotland to a new custodian and will hopefully be seen at many club events. Unless they were carefully managed equitably they schemed together and invariably sulked without lavish praise on a regular basis. Both cars display their Edwardian roots not least in the famous flat twin engine with its thermo syphon cooling.

A brief tech appendix for GET 898

79.4 × 101.6 produces 25 bhp with a CR of 5.4 to 1. Three-speed box allows excellent hill climbing ability albeit at tortoise speeds. (Please note that even Clarkson recently purchased a new tortoise). Less than 50 seconds to 50 mph and 30 mpg overall. 1951 price £525. 1952

This 1951 Bradford utility was bought by John and Barbara Atack from club member, Keith Wear, in 2003 who had owned it for many years. Keith's father originally owned from new the Bradford that was restored by Morrison's!

Bradford Ownership Today

Sadly, John died in 2015, but Barbara still owns the Bradford and takes it to local shows, she also attended the first ever Bradford-only rally in early May 2018 and the Jowett Car Club international rally in Harrogate over the late May bank holiday in 2018.

John and Barbara Atack regularly took the Bradford on continental trips, it was creating a lot of interest in the market square in Brest, France. (*Barbara Atack*)

price (double purchase tax) £740. Today, if you have a late model 4 litre XJS you could still swap it for a Bradford by only paying modest cash adjustment in part exchange. But don't scoff … ask about hill climbing with 7 cwt in the back!

Bill Bury—*Bill's Everyday Jowett Bradford*

It was 1960 when Bill Bury began his extraordinary love affair with a Jowett Bradford, that was destined for the scrapheap—but somehow never quite made it.

Morecambe man Bill was working in a scrapyard at the time when in came the nine-year-old Jowett Bradford estate, its engine at the end of its tether (likewise the owner!). A deal was struck, and Bill handed over a crisp new £5 note for the battered Bradford—and approximately 250,000 miles later (approximately the distance to the moon and back) they are inseparable.

The Bradford, now just on its third engine, is used daily. The 10 cwt capacity estate has carried beer kegs, diving gear, tents, clothes and food (yes—all at once!), it regularly tows a caravan and can be seen chugging around deepest Lancashire taking gradients in its stride. Of course, it was built before the phase 'built in obsolescence' was even thought of! Top speed says Bill is 70 mph, but she will pootle about at 50 mph all day.

Practically every panel has at some time been repaired or replaced, but Bill, a member of the Lakeland Historic Car Club and the Jowett Car Club, just carries out maintenance as and when it's necessary—he's never stooped to a full restoration!

Just after he bought the Bradford, his son was born, and Bill brought him home from hospital in the back of the Bradford estate. Last year his son's first daughter was born, and she too came back home in the Jowett.

Not so much a motor car—more a member of the family!

The Autojumbler 1989

I was talking to Bill in March 2018, and he is now an active 83-year-old who still owns his Bradford! He used to use it on a daily basis to take him to work at an oil refinery in Heysham where he was the in-house fire engine driver; he also serviced other lorries and vehicles on site. He is, of course, retired now and the Bradford also has a more leisurely lifestyle! (I still don't know how he got 70 mph out of it—50ish is the best I can do)!

Steve Waldenberg—Editor of our club magazine *The Jowetteer* 1985–1993

Steve was the editor of the club magazine, *The Jowetteer*, and ran a Bradford Utility for many years, he told me:

Bradford Ownership Today

Bill Bury has owned his 1951 Bradford utility since 1960, paying the princely sum of £5 for it after seeing it in a scrapyard. He used it as his daily transport to work for many years. Bill is now 83 years old. This picture, taken in the mid-1980s proves that a Bradford can tow a caravan! (*Bill Bury*)

Another view of Bill Bury's 1951 Bradford utility which is now in retirement so only attends rallies etc., it has also acted as a wedding car. (*Bill Bury*)

I did the Trans-Pennine road run several times, always driving over to my late friend John Charlton the day before, staying overnight and then proceeding to the start. On one occasion driving the 'old route' from Leeds—via Huddersfield, Holmfirth, Holme Moss, Glossop, etc. to Crewe I was driving up Holme Moss. Now we all know Bradfords have a very low ratio 1st gear and mine was in the habit of jumping out as the gears would be spinning quite fast, even at a sedate 5–6 mph. There was no reason to try to go any faster as 2nd gear would not pull it up the steep incline, so I just keep it in 1st keep my left hand on the gear lever and plod up. Well on this particular day there must have been a cycle race as several cyclists passed me on the uphill section!

You also had to beware long downhill sessions. If you attempted to keep speed down by brakes alone, one's foot would soon be at the floor boards as the drum brakes heated up and expanded—with a consequent loss of braking as the rods would only move so far. It was a case of keeping in 1st and 'sailing down' at no more than 8 or 9 mph or use 2nd gear and keep dabbing the brakes on and off to allow them to cool a little.

On one of the CD runs, Phill Green drove the van. He enjoyed his drive and after I dropped him back at Morrisons to retrieve his car. I proceeded home via Leeds ring road, then at the Spen Lane traffic lights just as I prepared to move off, there was a tremendous BANG and no power, I coasted to side of road. Upon lifting the bonnet, it was not a pleasant sight. The engine had completely destroyed itself, the crank case split in several pieces and oil all over the roadway. This then required a RAC recovery home and I had to source another engine. Sometime later, on another run the gearbox gave out on the hills approaching Hawes. A Javelin owner (NOC 11) attempted to tow me off but it needed a push from several members to get it moving. On the downhill stretch to Hawes I had to 'rely' on the brakes and it was not long before my foot was near the floor. I had to flash lights and gesticulate out of the window with my right arm and Martin (can't remember his surname) stopped and I nearly ran into him. I realised I had 2nd and top gear, so managed to run down to Hawes in 2nd gear. Then called RAC for a lift home. Bill Bury provided me with a rebuilt gearbox.

This was to me the last straw, so I sold the Bradford (to the same Martin) and put the money towards a Javelin. I bought the Bradford in 1984 and eventually sold it in 1993 when I got the red Javelin registered KTM 111.

N.B. Phill Green worked in the Experimental Department at Jowetts and drove one of the prototype Bradford CD's on a test run daily for several months. The CD Run was started by Steve Waldenberg in the 1980s re-enacting part of the original route, which also includes a high tea!

Steve Waldenberg was the editor of the Jowett Car Club newsletter, *The Jowetteer*, from 1985 to 1993 and during this period he owned this Bradford registered GBL 889 which was sign-written Jowett Car Club publicity department! This picture of Steve was taken in the Yorkshire Dales in the late 1980s.

Another view of Steve Waldenberg's Bradford registered GBL 889, this picture was taken on the Trans Pennine Run in 1984.

Bill & Sandra Purves

Bill's love affair with his 1947 Bradford registered LS 4878 began in 1979 when he was persuaded to buy it by fellow club member, Dennis Cremer. The Bradford was being disposed of by the Myreton Motor Museum where Dennis had his Jowett Javelin Convertible on display. Bill did not want a Bradford at that time as he was rebuilding his first car a 1934 Jowett named Belinda, but after some gentle encouragement he splashed-out £25.00 for it. This remained as the vehicle used in his business, 'Mr. Purves' Oil Lamp Emporium, Edinburgh,' until his death in 2016, by which time it is estimated that he had covered well in excess of 300,000 miles.

Following a very bad crash on the M6 when a tanker ploughed into the Bradford and trailer in 2000, it was eventually rebuilt to a very high standard by the late Roger Young and put back on the road in 2006. Since then it has been awarded many trophies at events all over the UK. In the M6 smash Sandra was thrown out of the van with only a fractured wrist but Bill was hospitalised. A brain scan the following morning highlighted a slight irregularity. Problems arose in 2004 when he suffered a mini-stroke, which he recovered from very quickly but was put on medication for life. In March 2009, he suffered his first stroke which was identified promptly but he was hospitalised again. He recovered well enough to take the Bradford to the JCC rally at Bideford in the May despite being told not to drive for more than two hours at any given time. He compromised by reducing it to seven hours!

Sandra remembers so many stories relating to their epic trips in the Bradford, such as attending the club rally in Paignton in 1985, followed by partaking in the London to Brighton Commercial Vehicle the next day having driven up to London overnight. Any sign saying, 'unsuitable for motor vehicles' became an instant challenge for Bill. Or the time they broke a con-rod on the Friarton Interchange, Perth which required a phone call to the RAC. They insisted it had to be a Bedford but had to agree it was a Bradford when the breakdown truck arrived!

On returning from the 800-mile round trip to the Jowett Car Club rally in Tewkesbury in 2016, on which journey he insisted on doing all the driving, Bill suffered a massive stroke which he never recovered from.

Sandra has kept in touch with the club, helping to run the international rally at Peebles in 2017 and attending our international rally in Harrogate in May 2018, and she still owns the Bradford and 1934 saloon. She is at the moment, arranging to display them at the Transport Museum in Dundee.

Bradford Ownership Today

Bill & Sandra Purves have owned this 1947 Bradford six-light utility since 1979. This must be one of the best-known Bradfords in the country, as they have travelled huge distances in it (in excess of 300,000 miles) to attend events all over the country. Sadly, Bill died in 2016 but Sandra still has it and attended our international rally in Peebles in it in May 2017.

Another view of Sandra Purves' 1947 Bradford six-light—note the interesting rear door opening

BJX 400 A Nostalgia Buy—Roger Learmonth

With a small and modest collection of old motors, I've rather majored on sporting Jaguars, from an SS100 to a Series 3 E Type. One or two other marques like an American Auburn Speedster and a Lagonda LG6 drop head also take up a bit of space but one of my most cherished charges is a Bradford lorry. Built on the same chassis as the van and utility, this wonderful example of British post-war austerity typifies the period perfectly. The term minimalist sums it up nicely; it has all the bits needed to stop and go but only just enough of each for it to happen.

I've owned my Braddie since 2003 and what started as a nostalgia buy has turned into something of a love affair. When I was a boy, my late father acquired a decrepit van for a tenner. His plan was elegant in its simplicity; buy it, do it up and flog it; ideally for a good profit. Sadly, the project turned out to be something of a disaster but, I suppose, the seed was sown. When we moved to our current house and saw the London to Brighton Commercial Run rumble past the top of our lane, the notion of joining in the fun was irresistible. If I was to acquire commercial however, what else could it be but a Bradford.

I like to try and be different so when, not a van nor a utility but a neat looking lorry, came up for sale, I grabbed my chance. With my nine-year-old daughter Elizabeth we did our first L2B in 2004 and have entered nearly every year since.

I have tried to keep the old lady as original as practical but will admit to taking a few liberties. We had continual problems with the six-volt electrics. I'm sure I could have persevered but when I was told that the later Jowett commercials featured twelve-volt electrics, I gave in and upgraded all the parts required. I can happily report that we have had no problems in that area since. Wandery [sic] steering was a tougher issue to resolve. I have to admit that taking to the road for the first time wasn't a bunch of fun; keeping her on the straight and narrow required rather a lot of effort. Renewing steering and suspension joints helped but, based on some sage advice, I reversed the front axle wedges which had an amazing effect on the geometry. Radial tyres completed the transformation, she now runs straight and true. The cab and truck bed have always been good, but I have treated her to major repairs of the coach-built doors and a comprehensive repaint. The all-wood bed was sanded down and treated to an enduring polyurethane finish; the metal fixings have been shot blasted and power coated.

Now for the bits that the purists may find distressing. I am led to believe that Jowett, in their wisdom, were prepared to offer any reasonable specification demanded by a customer and, of course, for which he or she was prepared to pay. I therefore set about converting my very basic lorry into a deluxe version. I don't know if any trucks left the factory that way but at least one now exists. My dear old BJX 400 sports a chromed radiator shell and chromium plated headlights as well as hubcaps. The seats, which had become rather down at heel, are now trimmed in complementary matching leather. We had a skilled sign writer carefully pinstripe the bonnet and doors. Two of my daughters occasionally drive her to shows and the rather whimsical signage gets a few laughs—'Learmonth & Daughters, Rag and Bone Girls'.

There are still few things to do but I think she looks a picture, but then I would, wouldn't I?

Roger Learmonth has a collection of several cars including sporting Jaguars and a Lagonda, in 2003 he succumbed to the charms of a Bradford lorry which he has owned ever since. He has regularly entered the Bradford in the London to Brighton commercial vehicle run with his daughter Lizzie, this is her during the 2004 run. (*R. Learmonth*)

This is Lizzie Learmonth during the 2013 London to Brighton Commercial Vehicle Run. (*R. Learmonth*)

I like the signwriting on the sides of the Learmonth Bradford! (*R. Learmonth*)

John & Danuta Morgan

John and Danuta Morgan have run the Jowett Car Club shop since 2009 selling club regalia including caps, fleeces, polo shirts, ties, car badges, key fobs, handbooks and literature etc. They often attend Jowett events, such as our international rallies with the shop so that members have a chance to purchase these items, they also offer a mail order service with their stock listed on the club's website. I asked John & Danuta if they would like to write something for the book, and this is what John has written for me:

> In approximately 1996, I saw a Bradford van for sale in the *Classic Car Weekly* newspaper in Peter Rogers' sale room in Huddersfield, who is well-known in Jowett circles, as he always has Jowetts in stock. I rang him, but it didn't come to pass. But a few months later I saw one advertised in Crickhowell, near Abergavenny, so I went to see it with my friend Obi, and I bought it. Then for several years it just languished in the garage.
>
> Then my darling Danuta and I got married, and she saw the Bradford under a sheet and said, 'what's that under there?' When I took off the cover she said, 'my god it's a Jowett Bradford!' I was shocked that she knew what it was. Then she said, 'don't you think it's about time you restored it?'
>
> So, in January 2000 we set to work, my friend Dave helped me, and Obi did the electrics, I completely remade the ash frame as I am a joiner by trade. When all complete it was time to start her up and away she went, it was then that we realised that the cylinders were cracked, this is when Martin Benning, a fellow Jowett Car Club member, came to the rescue. She was then resprayed sign written (John Morgan joinery, Newport).

Above: John & Danuta Morgan have run the Jowett Car Club shop since 2009, their Bradford van registered KVE 206 is a regular attendee at our club rallies. This picture was taken in 2016 at our rally in Tewksbury

Below: Another view of the Bradford of John and Danuta Morgan in Tewksbury in 2016.

By May, after all this work had been done she was ready for the long journey to Scotland (a 900-mile round trip), to take part in the Jowett Car Club international rally in Pitlochry. We set off on Tuesday and met up with other Jowett Car Club members and travelled up in convoy. She made it there and back with only a few hiccups.

She is my pride and joy and I couldn't be without her.

Harry Larcombe with the oldest known Bradford—plus others!

A piece appeared in *The Jowetteer* in May 1992 saying that, club member, Ian Aitken-Kemp owned the oldest surviving Bradford on the club register. It is chassis number D6/CA/915, and when Ian bought this from a number plate dealer its body had disintegrated or collapsed leaving the cab with no back to it.

It was owned from new by a Mr I. R. P. Heslop who was the district officer in Ikeja, Nigeria, where he ran the Bradford. It had the Nigerian registration number A3902. When he retired back to Burnham-on-Sea in Somerset in 1952, he brought the Bradford back with him. It was then re-registered in the UK NKA 910, Ian had the original receipt, dated 24 October 1946, for the vehicle which shows the purchase price of £387 which included various alterations which included repainting it in a two-tone colour scheme and fitting expanded metal mesh over the rear six windows—these were for security reasons to stop locals and monkeys from pilfering! It also had running boards fitted, which Ian thought were unique to this Bradford.

My friend, Harry Larcombe, who lives only eight miles away from me near Whitby, bought the Bradford from Ian some time ago and plans to restore it, but he intends to make it into a lorry, as there is no surviving bodywork beyond the bonnet and cab.

At the moment he is working on his ultra-rare Bradford ice cream van, which also appears in this book, the mechanicals have been restored but work still needs to be carried out to the bodywork. He also owns a Bradford van which was owned by the publishing company, Bay View Books, it still carries this livery and looks very smart. This van attended the first ever Bradford only rally in Buxton in May 2018. Another gem in his collection is a little red Bradford lorry which was originally supplied new to the Jowett agents, North Riding Motors of York, where it was used by them as the garage hack. It still carries the North Riding Motors livery and is a little beauty!

Harry is a real Jowett fan, and has several other Jowetts in his collection besides the Bradfords listed above.

Harry Larcombe has a large collection of Jowetts including four Bradfords, this ultra-rare ice cream van is being worked on at the moment, the engine has been restored but the bodywork still needs a considerable amount of work.

Harry Larcombe bought this 1953 Bradford registered PYB 385 from Bay View Books, a motoring publisher, it is still in the same livery at the moment.

This is a really smart 1949 lorry that is in Harry Larcombe's collection, it was owned from new by the Jowett agents, North Riding Motors, based in York.

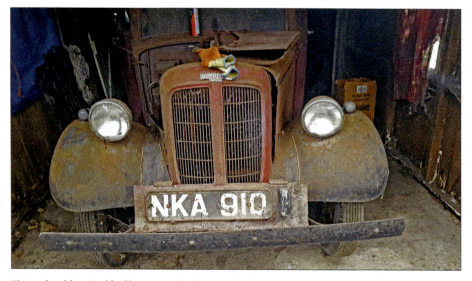

This is the oldest Bradford known to the Club, a 1946 CA example, it is now part of Harry Larcombe's collection. It is in a poor condition and incomplete, but I hope one day this will also be restored, as it is a historic vehicle.

Jack Moon

The Jowett Car Club was contacted in 2014 by a long-time Jowett owner, Ray Milton, as he wanted somebody within the club to take his Bradford van and restore it as it had been parked-up for over 50 years and he wanted to see it back on the road again. I am pleased to say that one of our younger members, Jack Moon, took up the challenge and is doing a great job with it, as his account shows:

The first ever Bradford weekend in May 2018 seemed like too good a deadline to get her on the road, confirmed with some gentle encouragement from Mr Brown and Mr Gregg, and the chance to see Staden Grange, its alpacas and the project Bradford in the garage for the first time and put my tent up was too good to miss.

With a few months to go, it soon became very clear I had nowhere near enough time to finish lots of even the important jobs that were required before heading 170 miles north in a Bradford that had managed little more than 40 miles since 1964.

After months of minor adjustments, a reconditioned steering box, adjustments to brakes, chasing rattles and squeaks, and a couple of short test drives, the weather forecast looked tremendous (if a bit hot for a Bradford which had no track record of driving a long distance and not boiling over) and so we set off bright and early on Friday with lots of tools, oil, water and fingers crossed.

Progress was good, oil pressure was good, water temperature remained sensible, and I was starting to feel quite confident of an easy drive and arriving in time to erect the tent and enjoy dinner in the local pub, until I reached Towcester and just down the A5 with a queue of bank holiday traffic behind me I tried to change down from third gear to tackle a hill and found the gearbox refusing to let me out of third gear at all. Round 1 knockout blow, just 60 miles completed, or so it seemed, while I crawled to a layby, swearing quite a lot.

At this point Facebook earned its worth in minutes, with an update posted, and suddenly input on potential fixes was coming from across the UK (along with some unhelpful input from other friends who thought I was mad to attempt it in the first place!) and photos instantly shared of the inside of the troublesome gearbox, but special thanks goes to Richard Turner, Alan Bartlett and David Mason for advice and encouragement while I waited for Mr RAC to come and hold my spanners for me!

Soon a fair amount of wear was diagnosed, but removing the top, pushing the ring back, and then driving while holding the gearstick up as high as possible to keep it from slipping too far and jamming seemed to do the trick, for 40 minutes. Cue a large roundabout and trying to escape to a lay-by in third gear for another strip down, before deciding that I was going to make it, no matter what. All went fine for another 2.5 hours and then two miles from dinner she stuck fast again at 7 p.m. on a very steep hill! Luckily, I arrived, to a round of applause, just before starters were served and Steve Gray joined me for the crawl home from the pub in first and second gear to the campsite to begin an enjoyable weekend.

Discretion being the better part of valour, I accepted the offer of a lift to the days out, which included great fun at Steeple Grange Light Railway (where our esteemed editor John Cash and other volunteers were very welcoming and knowledgeable) and the Ecclesbourne Valley Railway, riding a steam train up the hill from Wirksworth station, and a trip to Duffield before heading back to Staden Grange for a couple of hours of gearbox surgery with input from almost everyone (and hands-on help from several enthusiastic volunteers) to find at least a bodge solution that would avoid a trip home on a low loader!

The Crich tramway museum was a great location for a relaxed day in the sunshine showing off the Bradfords to the public, some local friends were fascinated with our 'funny old cars' but the gearbox work was waiting for me and a 7 p.m. dinner deadline would not be missed! With seconds to spare, the bodge gearbox fix was completed without removal being required and the test drive to the pub proved uneventful, with Paul Beumont encouraging some entirely irresponsible speeds from the passenger seat to make sure third gear really wasn't going to stick on the way home.

It would have been cowardly not to test my handiwork on a 170-mile test drive home, so the decision was made and I packed up the tools ready for the hottest May bank holiday on record, safe in the knowledge the RAC was on speed dial just in case, and I had water and snacks to keep me going if I needed them—luckily an uneventful seven-hour drive ensued, and the old girl was safe and sound in time for dinner and a very early night!

A huge thanks is due to Tim Brown, Alastair Gregg, and everyone involved in making this event such a success. With a dozen Bradfords visiting it is as many as I have ever seen in one place, and we are all looking forward to this event next year and seeing more Bradfords join us for a relaxed and thoroughly enjoyable weekend. Many commented how many sections were represented, I spent a lot of time with members I had not met before and others who I had not had the chance to enjoy socialising with as much as I should have and learned plenty about Bradfords which will be invaluable in the coming years.

William Calvert—Calvert's Carpets Publicity Bradford Lorry

One Saturday morning about thirty years ago a cheque came in the post from my late grandfather's estate for a few hundred pounds, similar payments were made to each of his grandchildren. I always remembered him having a Bradford and calling in to see us with it as a child.

That Saturday night we were going out to see some friends just outside Leeds where we stayed the night, waking up the next morning nursing a rather sore head I walked up the lane where they lived and there was a very sad looking Bradford on someone's drive whereupon I knocked on this chap's door and ended up buying it from him with some of grandad's money!

It then lived in my yard for years and I was always going to do it up (restore) but never did. Later we moved it into a barn where I totally forgot all about it.

Jack Moon's 1951 Bradford registered NAR 744 after its epic trip of 170 miles to the Bradford rally in Buxton in May 2018.

Jack Moon with his 1951 Bradford registered NAR 744 in the rally hotel car park in Buxton in May 2018.

William Calvert owns Calvert's Carpets having over a dozen stores including Northallerton, Middlesbrough, Scarborough and York. He has owned this 1950 Bradford lorry for approximately thirty years and uses it for publicity in his shops. (*W. Calvert*)

Another picture of William Calvert's 1950 Bradford lorry registered MTU 134. (*W. Calvert*)

I had to show this picture of the Calvert's Carpets Bradford, as my son, Jonathan, had gone into one of the Calvert's Carpets stores about ten years ago to buy some carpets and had the shock of his life when he spotted the Bradford as part of the display in the shop! (*Jonathan Stokoe*)

Many years later on my Birthday my two sons came and picked me up to go for a beer and on the way stopped at an industrial unit outside Thirsk. One of my sons went inside and then shouted for us two to come in where the Bradford stood there restored what a shock that was! Since then we've only used it in store for promotional purposes.

The Young Family

Roger Young will be forever remembered with great affection by members of the Jowett Car Club, he was a Bradford man through and through. Sadly, he died very suddenly on 17 August 2010 which must have been devastating to his family and to many club members alike (me included).

I well-remember the great excitement he caused by arriving at the club's centenary rally in Wakefield in May 2010 with his wife, Carol, and daughters Sara and Rachel in a large Volvo car transporter with three concours Bradfords on board and towing a Jowett stationary engine! I, like many others, ran over with my camera to capture this unique moment. All three of these Bradfords had been totally restored to a very high standard and all took concours prizes at the rally! His collection of concours Bradfords amounted to four, as in the sales booklet, 'Jowett's famous four Bradfords'.

Roger also restored Bradfords for club members, the most notable being the well-known and much-loved 'Lamp Emporium' Bradford of Bill & Sandra Purves of Edinburgh. They had a devastating crash on the M6 on the way to a club rally. They had been hit by a speeding HGV driver who had fallen asleep at the wheel. Bill was seriously injured but Sandra escaped with minor injuries. Their Bradford was written-off by the insurance company as the body had disintegrated. Bill passed the wreck to Roger, who was able to restore it in time for Bill & Sandra to take it to the club's international rally in Crieff in 2009.

Just before the 2010 centenary rally John Morgan's Bradford was badly damaged when a lady drove into the side of him. Roger managed to replace and repair the damaged timberwork and body panels and re-sprayed it just in time for the rally. Both of these Bradfords are featured in this book, as both are to concours standard, and are a testament to Roger's skill and expertise.

I am delighted to say that Roger's collection of four restored Bradfords are still owned by his wife Carol, and daughter's Rachel and Sara. They still enter rallies on a regular basis, Sara and Rachel attended the club's international rally in Harrogate with the 1951 utility registered BCW 144 and won the concours again with it!

This wonderful picture was taken at the Jowett Car Club centenary rally in Wakefield in May 2010 which Roger Young together with his wife, Carol and daughters Rachel and Sara arrived. What better way to transport three Bradfords and a Jowett stationary engine! The three Bradfords were later driven to the concours site by Roger, Rachel and Sara—she was 17 at the time and just passed her driving test!

Bradford Ownership Today

The four Bradfords owned by the Young family, a 1952 lorry registered CCN 112, 1953 van registered SPG 525, 1947 van registered KKX 685 and 1951 utility registered BCW 144, Carol Young is in the centre with Sara and Rachel. (*Young*)

Sara and Rachel Young with the four Bradfords. (*Young*)

The four Young family Bradfords. (*Young*)

Sara Young at the wheel of one of the Bradfords with Rachel. (*Duncan Pound*)

Tim Brown—1947 Utility registered JPO 827

Tim is a true stalwart of the Jowett Car Club and has owned numerous Jowetts over the years, and still has a good collection of them today—including a Bradford. This particular Bradford was rescued by Tim in 2017 and was reported in several of the *Classic Car* magazines, this is what the January 2018 issue of *Classic & Sportscar* had to say:

> Tim Brown of Congleton recently discovered a 1947 Bradford Utility which he had heard about via the Jowett Car Club. A widow had wanted to sell the vehicle which had been in a leaking garage for 30-years.
>
> 'Her husband appears to have been a bit of a hoarder,' said Brown, 'never throwing anything away. This was evident upon first visiting the Utility, which had to be unearthed to see it properly.' The Jowett looked complete, so Brown bought it.
>
> All that is known of its history is that it was sold new by Marriot's Garage, Worthing and has the Sussex registration JPO 827.

The Bradford was restored in record time by Chris Spencer of *Flat Cap Classic Cars* to concours standard just in time for Tim to take it on the first ever Bradford-only rally based in Buxton, which he was organising (see below). The Bradford went on to win the Premier Concours Award at the Jowett Car Club international rally in Harrogate in May 2018, which was well-deserved as it looks fantastic!

This is description of the Bradford rally that he arranged:

> A chance remark over 12 months ago at a North West Section meeting propagated a desire to hold and arrange an exclusive meeting for Bradfords as it was generally held that (rightly or wrongly) they enjoyed a lower profile than other manifestations of our marque. Contemporarily it seems that demand for Bradfords is at an all-time high and demand for road-worthy examples is outstripping supply.
>
> But many project examples are regularly emerging from the undergrowth of people's gardens where they have been literally abandoned 30 to 50 years ago. If the chassis of those are sound it is possible to execute a rebuild with a plentiful supply of spares and knowhow within our club.
>
> It should also be not forgotten that around 40,000 Bradfords were built and survivors are apparent around the world and their numbers of production I think exceeds the total of all other examples of the Jowett marque. The Bradford was the nation's tireless workhorse in the austerity years following WW2. The revenue derived from Bradford sales kept Jowett Cars Ltd motoring as none of the other post-war production (Javelin and Jupiter) was profitable.
>
> A decision was therefore made to go ahead and organise an exclusive Bradford meeting which was centred on Staden Grange Hotel, Buxton, Derbyshire owned by Bradford (and Jupiter!) owner Alastair Gregg and we managed to attract a gathering of 11 Bradfords

comprising utilities, utility deluxe, vans and lorries in the ownerships of Steven Gray, Glyn Davies, Jack Moon, David Mason, Paul Beaumont, Barbara Atack, Harry Larcombe, Paul Rennie, Richard Rhodes, Alastair Gregg and Tim Brown plus Bill Lock and Noel Stokoe in inferior vehicles! Of course, all were accompanied by their wives/companions/girlfriends. The whole weekend was blessed with wall to wall sunshine and only two retardations; an element of fuel starvation and gearbox misdemeanour but both were ingeniously rectified with much opinion and suggestion from everyone as you can imagine!

Pauline Brown acted as shotgun with the Subaru carrying spares, tow ropes, tools and fuel and really played a blinder in following the troupe round the Peak District.

From feedback received the event was a resounding success and discussion will ensue within the North West Section as to whether we should do it again next year. Finally, huge thanks to all who brought and drove their Bradfords to this meeting and thanks to Alastair for making us very welcome.

Tim Brown's latest Jowett restoration project, a 1948 utility registered JPO 827, being dragged out of the damp garage it had been stored in for over thirty years.

Above and below: Tim Brown's 'as found' Bradford at Chris Spencer's workshops ready for restoration. (*Flat Cap Classics*)

(*Image courtesy of Tim Brown*)

The restored Bradford of Tim Brown, ready just in time to take part in the Bradford-only rally in Buxton that Tim had organised.

David & Sue Mason—and Percy!

A 1951 CB Bradford van, registered AEN 853 was purchased by us in November 1997 for £500 as a partly restored project from a man in Rotherham, whose wife had given him an ultimatum. The owner was a heavy-goods wagon driver and we arranged for him to bring it on his low loader to the restoration garage, located in Biddulph, near Congleton. The day arrived when the project was being delivered: it snowed, but the man, straight out of the Yorkie advert, trundled up having crossed the Pennines in a blizzard and braved the traffic. The van was unloaded, and we shook hands, but as he was driving off, he stopped the wagon, called me over and spoke these words 'it's called Percy and I haven't bothered to change it' and so at that moment Percy was born.

I don't think the garage had any experience in restoring wood-framed commercial vehicles, but for the grand sum of £1,660 Percy was smartened up and ready to go. We ran him in his green livery with no lettering, and in fact handed him over to our son as his first vehicle when he learned to drive.

The van was a work-horse, mainly used for taking stuff to the local recycling and collecting plants from the Garden Centre though it has attended at least two national Jowett rallies.

When our son left for London and University, we took the opportunity to have Percy's ID put on the van, so we approached Malcolm Barker, Jowett owner and member in Stamford to make us the lettering that declares, 'Percy the Bradford'.

Above and below: Two views of 'Percy' David & Sue Mason's 1951 van.

A most memorable outing for Percy was to take our son to a local wedding, though the wedding present of a cheque in an envelope, slid off the seat and down a crack under the door and out into the road. It was found by a passing cyclist whose wife was the registrar and who told him where the names on the envelope were getting married. So, a man in Lycra popped up at the wedding with the cheque.

Other highlights have including taking it to the tip with rubbish and being informed that it was a commercial vehicle and, therefore, a fee was due. Challenging this with the local council the official told us she was rubbish with classic vehicles!

Percy has never let us down. Occasional fuel starvation issues have been the only mechanical glitches in 21 years, but Jowett Car Spares came up with a new pump which has solved the problem.

Maurice Benning with GAB 592

First sold from Jowett dealers Williams of Pierpoint Street, Worcester in 1947 to Mr Alex Wheeler (Evesham & then Broadway), who happened to be a beekeeper. When he thought it would fail its MOT, he sold it to my Dad in 1956, who was also a beekeeper and knew it would hold six hives and was useful for moving them between sites. On several occasions I went with him to tend to the bees and one time they took a liking to me and I ended up covered in iodine, while dad only ever used a veil as he said you became immune after a while! It never did fail its MOT. In fact, in later years a tester couldn't understand why foot and hand brakes were so good (rod system).

I remember, when young a lot of 'camping' holidays in Wales—if it rained in the north we went south and vice versa. With seats moved forward, my younger sister slept across the front seat, me across the back, with Dad & Mum in the rear with the doors open a homemade 'platform' with two drop-down legs and canvas across the top.

One trip took us over horseshoe pass, with dad pausing at the top with the comment 'you have five minutes for photos & then we are going'—to cool GAB on the way down the other side.

The village of Hinton on the Green lies split across the River Isbourne, with steep banks either side. Dad was checking, the brakes on one occasion & mum went with him in the passenger seat. As he went down the bank, he applied the brakes and mum ended up in the foot-well. All Dad said was 'they'll do then'!

When restoration became necessary in the early 80s, Colin Angell (who lived in and had restored Hinton Mill) offered one of his outbuildings for Dad to use, otherwise, it would have been done on the side of the road, where it was parked permanently. He rebuilt the ash frame, hand brush painted it—Valspar Battleship grey and along with mum (seat recovering), elder brothers Mick (mechanic) and Maurice (bodyshop), GAB re-took to the road in 1983/4(?).

Above and below: Two views of Maurice Benning's 1947 'six-light' registered GAB 592

In 1987, he took it to the Jowett national rally in Welshpool (camping —but this time in a tent). Brother Malcolm and I with our wives also went. On the scenic run, the ladies sat on the back seat while Malcolm and I sat on the wheel arches. Dad decided 'you young ones like to drive fast' so went 'careering' around the Welsh lanes making it not scenic, more uncomfortable! He did enjoy that rally, especially meeting up with friend and another 'Bradford' man the late Bill Purves of 'The Lighting Emporium' fame.

After dad died in 1990, ownership passed over to brothers Mick and Maurice jointly, so has remained since leaving its birthplace, GAB has remained in Worcestershire.

Over recent years there has been a growing interest in Bradfords overseas, particularly in Australia and New Zealand, where new restorations are taking place on a regular basis. Here are just a few of the stories I could have used from Australia and New Zealand:

Bill Ebzery—Wait And See—Australia

Bill, in my opinion, is a true living legend and has done more to publicise the Bradford in Australia than anybody else I can think of—he is a hero of mine! I had the pleasure of meeting him and his wife, Susan, when they attended our centenary rally in Bradford in 2010. For many years Bill ran a Javelin as his main family transport vehicle which he rescued from a quarry in Wagga Wagga and restored. Bill, like most people, regarded the Bradford as an 'agricultural vehicle' that basically fell apart as the ash timbers dried out in the Australian sun and collapsed, and not really worth saving. This all changed, however, when he attended the Jowett national rally in 1998 at Burra, South Australia, when he met Brian Hehir (mentioned by me a little later). Brian had driven a round-trip of over 6,763 km (4,200 miles), to attend the rally which included crossing the Nullarbor Plain, 1,190 km long (739 miles)! To cut a very long story short, Bill and Susan collected the remains of at least six Bradfords abandoned in barns and fields etc. across Australia. Bill and his team then rebuilt them into three 1949 Bradford lorries. The Bradfords were then sign written WAIT, AND, SEE in memory of the WAIT & SEE Jowetts that crossed Africa in 1926. Bill and his team then undertook a remarkable trip with these Bradfords by crossing Australia West to East from Perth to Sydney.

The Bradfords were then transported to York in Western Australia in August 2008 which was 96 km (59 miles) from Perth on the west coast. The Bradfords drove into Perth for a couple of days and went to the Freemantle Sailing Club so that they could dip their front wheels into the Indian Ocean at the start of their epic trek east to Sydney. The team comprised of Bill Ebzery, Susan Sharrock, Robert Rowley, Rosalie Hefferman, Howard Norfolk, Ollie Stevenson and Barry Harding. They arrived twenty-four days later in Sydney after covering a total of 5,287 km (3,285 miles). The team then went to the slipway at Rose

Bay, where Bill, his son and grandson poured the Indian Ocean water down the slipway to join the Pacific Ocean.

The team had some great adventures during the crossing, covering an average of 220 km a day (137 miles), which included a race round the famous Mount Panorama race track at Bathurst where the three Bradfords took eleven minutes to complete a lap. The official lap record there in a supercar is just over two minutes, but this time of eleven minutes, of course, is a world record for a Bradford. Another world record claimed was for changing the rear axle of one of the Bradfords at the side of the road in two hours!

Bill published an excellent book and DVD called *The Wait And See Odyssey* in 2009, which is compulsive reading and viewing to Jowett fans.

This was not the end of Bill's epic trips, as he arranged the *Bradford 1000* where Wait And See and two other Bradfords drove approximately 200 km a day from Lockhart, NSW to attend the Jowett Car Club of Australia national rally in Cowra, NSW on 8 April 2016.

Bill Ebzery had planned the epic crossing of Australia west to east in 2008 in these three restored Bradford lorries, Wait, And, See inspired by the crossing of Africa in 1926 in two Jowetts named Wait and See. Here are the three Bradfords dipping their wheels in the Indian Ocean at the start of the trip in Perth. (*Bill Ebzery*)

Wait And See at the end of their 'record breaking' lap round the famous Mount Panorama Race Track at Bathurst in eleven minutes. The record for a supercar is just over two minutes! (*Bill Ebzery*)

Journeys end, Bill Ebzery, his son and grandson empty the water they collected in Perth into the Pacific Ocean at Rose Bay near Sydney

Bill Ebzery and me at the Jowett Car Club centenary rally in Wakefield in 2010 (*Jane Stokoe*)

Bill Ebzery arranged the *Bradford 1000* where Wait And See and two other Bradfords drove approximately 200 km a day from Lockhart, NSW to attend the Jowett Car Club of Australia National Rally in Cowra, NSW on 8 April 2016. (*Bill Ebzery*)

A rear view of the five Bradfords on the Bradford 1000 run. (*Bill Ebzery*)

Tony George—Australia

I didn't actually go looking for a Bradford. I had finished the restoration of a Javelin and was part way into a similar exercise with a Jupiter. It was 1985 and I had the Javelin at a display when I was offered this Bradford by a chap who obviously knew the Jowett connection and 'wanted it to go to an enthusiast who would restore it and give it a good home'. I was still working then, and the Jupiter was taking any spare time I had. I didn't need anything more. But anything Jowett is worth saving and he lived nearby; no trouble to look. The price of which was no more than salvageable engine parts or a back axle. Someone somewhere would surely want these items. The deal was done.

As found, it wasn't pretty. Typically, the timber of the body framework had rotted to the stage of collapse and many body panels had fallen off. But the important ones like the cab, mudguards and bonnet were all there and mechanically it looked complete. It was trailered home and stored while work continued on the Jupiter.

Over time, the timber was dismantled and marked, fortunately most of the pieces being suitable for patterns. Other restorations came and were completed and by this time I was assisted by my able grandson Lawrie. Still the Bradford waited.

Fast forward to the Australian national Jowett rally of 2010 where revival of interest in Bradfords resulted in them almost outnumbering the Javelins present! Which then prompted the remark from Lawrie 'Hey Grandpa, what say we brush the cobwebs from the remains of our Bradford and drive it to the 2012 Rally in South Australia.' This was the trigger needed to clean the 25 years of dust off ours and try to have it ready for the rally. Two years! Was it possible, keeping in mind that at most we had one day a week available?

Lawrie bought a precision saw bench, armfuls of Tasmanian oak, made a finger-jointing jig and, with much gluing and laminating, we had a frame to original specification.

Happily, the engine needed nothing more than a valve grind and a set of big end shells and while on the mechanicals we decided to treat the Bradford—and ourselves!—to a bit of luxury and replaced the standard 3 speed gearbox with a 5 speed one. Well, it had been very patient!

What did become obvious at this stage was accident damage sometime in its earlier life. The van had been involved in a sideswipe on the passenger side. Filler by the bucket load in the mudguard and door. The original aluminium panel below the back windows it seems had been too crumpled to fix and had been replaced with a heavy steel one. A restorer's life is never dull!

Steadily it all came together but, like all restorations, not as quickly as we had would have liked. No time for testing; we had just 6 days for the 1,800-mile trip to Adelaide. It made it, won some awards at the rally and returned to Perth, covering 4,000 miles. Not bad for a light van designed for town deliveries. Ben and William built them tough. Did they have an inkling of what some Aussies would put them through 70 years on?

Tony George, April 2018

Tony George at the start of the 90-mile straight on the way to the Jowett Car Club rally in Adelaide, a 1,800-mile trip—each way! (*Tony George*)

Tony George's Bradford utility being admired at a classic car event. (*Tony George*)

Brian Hehir, Australia

My Bradford ownership was not planned. I was looking to gain experience in the restoration of timber-framed bodywork in preparation for restoring a pre-war Jowett tourer. When a Bradford lorry was advertised for sale in a local newspaper, the choice was obvious. The Bradford had experienced a hard life. Apart from the cab floor and back, most of the timberwork including the tray was missing. The chassis was bent but the engine ran and the brakes had been relined. The restoration was made difficult by the lack of local examples. The closest example of a complete Bradford was owned by Tony George and I am grateful for his assistance. I chose to laminate the timber of the windscreen pillars and doors. This was not the easiest method of construction and with the benefit of hindsight ignored the advances made in glue technology. In spite of this, the bodywork has remained intact for more than 20 years.

The restoration was to be a practical one which would maintain the appearance and features of the Bradford. After a lengthy process the vehicle was completed and licensed in 1997.

After driving the Bradford for approximately 500 km I felt that it could be driven across the Nullarbor Plain to the 1998 National Jowett Rally in Burra in South Australia. As I was still working and did not have time to drive the return journey I was accompanied by a support vehicle, driven by my brother-in-law Austin Risbey. The journey to Burra of 1,600 miles was successfully completed in six days. In 2000 the National Jowett Rally was in the coastal town of Rockingham, Western Australia, a comparatively short distance from home.

The following year the Bradford as an entrant in the Centenary of Federation Rally was driven to Canberra. Fellow Bradford enthusiast Barry Harding accompanied me on this rally and while in Canberra the decision was made to continue to Bateman Bay on the east coast of New South Wales. The Bradford had now been driven from the west coast to the east coast of Australia.

A major disaster occurred in 2006 on the way to the national Jowett rally in Armidale in New South Wales. The engine had run out of oil as a result of being driven too hard. It appears that the crankcase valve was responsible. Either the valve does not cope with continued vehicle speeds in excess of 45 mph, or the valve was faulty. Fortunately, we were able to deal with this situation. At Armidale, due to the generosity of a local freight company, Bill Ebzery, John Muhleisen and Neil Moore the Bradford was wheeled into the workshop at 9 a.m. and driven out at 6 p.m. that evening having been re-engined approx. 2,000 miles from home and on a public holiday. At the conclusion of the rally the Bradford was successfully driven back to Western Australia. This situation reflects the remarkable camaraderie which exists within the Jowett Car Club. In attending national Jowett rallies over 20 years and counting each way the Bradford has been driven across the Nullarbor Plain 12 times.

Some other trips:

In 2002 the Bradford was driven to Wellington in New South Wales, a round trip of approximately 5,000 miles in 5 weeks.

2004 Rally in Tasmania a distance of 7,000 miles was driven in 7 weeks.

2008—Bendigo Rally—4,266 miles in 25 days

2012—South Australian Rally—3,675 miles in 27 days

Generally, 250 miles a day is comfortable driving however, depending on circumstances, greater distances have been travelled.

Since 2012 the Bradford has been transported to national rallies by vehicle trailer.

Even though very few people have heard of a Bradford, it always attracts interest. The rugged simplicity of the Bradford enables it to perform well above perceived capabilities. The lack of a 4-speed gearbox and modest top speed do not make the Bradford ideal for long distance driving, but the lack of surprises caused by pressurised cooling and hydraulic systems is adequate compensation.

In retrospect, I regard my Bradford experiences as very rewarding. Many lessons have been learned and the door has been opened to many enjoyable opportunities.

I should mention the late Beryl Langley. She had a very nicely restored CB Bradford which was the best restored Bradford around for many years. Beryl was an enthusiast and is remembered for her willingness to share information and generous hospitality.

Brian Hehir restored this Bradford lorry to a very high standard, he is renowned in Australia for covering huge mileages in it to attend Club rallies etc. (*Brian Hehir*)

Another view of Brian Hehir's Bradford lorry. (*Brian Hehir*)

Doug Rath—Australia

Our Rath Bradford story started with a call from Brian Holmes, the then Jowett Car Club of Australia president. He said, 'how would you like to come and look at a Bradford'. Not wanting to disappoint him I agreed. It wasn't until later I realised I was being set up. The Bradford turned out to be the first work vehicle of 'Colac Electrical' Colac being a city about 150 km south west of Melbourne, Australia.

Our family being electricians, Brian knew that I would be a sucker for it, and naturally I bought the Bradford.

The little beast had had a restoration of sorts but needed some sorting out. Everything that was still original we decided to keep as it was, and only make it serviceable. It is so original that I believe it would be a great shame to restore it more than necessary. The only mechanical alteration has been a modern oil filter conversion and an electric fan, for use in traffic.

I have a selection of old tools that are kept in the tray, to add a little extra when the Bradford goes to a display. Ladder racks were made, old school and oregon ladders sourced, a tonneau cover was made for the rear and the original mud flaps restored and fitted. Sign writing was applied to the doors and tail gate in the old school. I hate to see computer generated stickers on classic vehicles, so the signs are painted on.

Our first outing in the Bradford was to the RACQ motoring of Yesteryear display, which we won in the commercial division. That was 1996. The Bradford won the best Bradford at the JCCA national rally in Armidale as well.

At our recent JCCA National Rally in Toowoomba a second-best Bradford was awarded. The first place going to a beautifully recently restored Bradford utility in bright red. In the run up to the recent rally in Toowoomba we placed the Bradford in the Toowoomba Cob & Co Museum on display. It looked great, and there were many admirers there and at the club display that weekend.

The Bradford is a mighty little truck as long as the driver is patient, and takes their time with gear changes etc. I would like to acknowledge the help of Brian Holmes, motor engineer extraordinaire and local Jupiter owner for his help and support with our family of Jowett vehicles.

The Bradford is kept company by our Jupiter and Javelin, so he is never lonely!

We intend using our Bradford more now that we live in the country and where there is a lot less traffic.

Where ever the Jowett club goes there is always a lot of interest in our vehicles and the Bradford is never left out. The crowd love them!

Doug Rath has restored this Bradford lorry in Australia, he also races his Jowett Jupiter. (*Doug Rath*)

Doug Rath's Bradford lorry attracting some attention. Unfortunately, I have never received this sort of attention with my Bradford! (*Doug Rath*)

Beryl Langley—Australia

Whilst contacting members in Australia I was asked by more than one person to mention Beryl Langley, she was a life member of the Jowett Car Club of Australia but died in August 2014 aged 91. Her late husband, Alick, restored a 1951 Bradford lorry which he bought in 1987 for A$600. Alick had retired in 1980 due to ill-health but relished the prospect of restoring the Bradford. The vehicle was completely stripped-down as much of the timberwork was either rotten or missing, and the wings were in a poor state also.

This Bradford is another example of a rolling chassis that had been supplied to Australia where a special body was fitted by the agents Liberty Motors of Melbourne. Beryl was in charge of the finance and her records showed that A$10,677.77 was spent in its restoration. Friends and family helped Alick more as his health failed. He had set the deadline for finishing it to attend the Jowett Car Club rally in Canberra in 1992. The Bradford was finished in time and Alick and Beryl returned with three main trophies from the weekend. Sadly, the event exhausted Alick and he collapsed when he returned home, he was taken to hospital, but never returned home.

Beryl remained a club member for the rest of her life, won numerous trophies, and was a source of help and inspiration to many people.

Beryl Langley's beautifully restored Bradford lorry which was bodied locally in Melbourne. Sadly, Beryl died in August 2014. The Bradford is pictured here as part of her funeral cortège. It is still owned by the family. (*Andrew Henshall*)

A Bradford by Jowett By Jove!—Vic Morrison New Zealand

In 1989 Maureen and I bought an old cottage in the country in a place called Whitecliffs. On one of the paddocks was a pile of rubbish, resembling a dump. I said to Maureen, 'what we need is a big truck to get rid of that rubbish.'

Now it so happened that tucked away in my Mum's garage was the mechanicals of a Bradford that I had saved from being dumped years before. I decided I would make a truck from these parts. It was to be a simple affair and based on the Australian bodied pick-up that they made for the drive-away chassis at the time, complete with a soft top but not a folding one. Once I had a rolling chassis work started on the body. It had the usual Bradford front and bulkhead, but I cut the windscreen pillars (these were damaged) and made my own screen with the aforementioned soft top. The pair of doors similarly had the window frames cut and capped along the top by wood. Hinged perspex was used for the side windows. I decided on a well side for the deck, for when the tailgate was dropped it increased the load space significantly as I had this pile of rubbish in mind. For the well sides I used oil tempered hardboard again capped by varnished wood in line with the doors.

Our Cottage in the country was to be a holiday retreat so I built up the Bradford from our home in Christchurch. Luckily the motor that came with it had been reconditioned by the previous owner and a good job he made of it too. This saved me time and money. Once mobile and registered and warranted its first run was to Whitecliffs, from where we made several fully-loaded trips to the local dump to get rid of all that rubbish. In 1992 we decided to live permanently at Whitecliffs having enjoyed most weekends and all holidays there. Now that little Bradford really came into its own as we moved all our furniture and belongings plus all my garage stuff in the back of the Bradford albeit making many trips. Our daughter came with us as she was still at school but our two boys were working by now, so they stayed in our Christchurch home. Eventually as Debbie grew up she too started work and later went flatting so the Bradford was used to move her stuff several times for as you know daughters come back home to live for a while, then off again. The Bradford coped with it all.

We had a little land around us at Whitecliffs and Maureen being keen on horses we had 12 miniature horses which meant there was a never-ending supply of manure to be raked or picked up. Along with this was the need for many bales of hay and the Bradford pulled the harrow, carted manure and gathered the hay from the surrounding area, year in year out. In 1999 we built a new house on our land and once again our little work-horse rose to the challenge carting the many building supplies notching up a round trip of nearly 100 miles each trip. Not only has it been a marvellous work-horse but what surprised me was how much fun it was to take on the many Jowett rallies we enjoyed in our Bradford and needing very little in the way of maintenance.

It has carried, sand, shingle, timber, fence posts, concrete curbing, hay (up to 20 bales with a special rack), manure etc., all very heavy and well over the rating. For some loads I had to tie the doors shut as there was a certain amount of flexing at times you understand! That gallant little twin cylinder just plodded on in its uncomplaining way with that reassuring exhaust beat they have.

Eventually we had to leave our beloved Whitecliffs and come back to Christchurch and yes, the Bradford shifted all our stuff once again. It gave us 29 wonderful years of service and it was with much regret that due to the need to downsize we sold our faithful servant. Luckily though it went to a Jowett enthusiast who loves it for what it is. Funnily enough he has just finished building a house and the Bradford has been pressed again into service to help with the build.

Above: Vic Morrison restored this Bradford lorry in New Zealand in 1989, he and his wife had bought a family retreat outside Christchurch, so it was used to transport their furniture etc to it. It had been a reliable little workhorse until he recently sold it to another Jowett enthusiast, Vic still has several other Jowetts. (*Vic Morrison*)

Below: Vic Morrison's Bradford lorry was bodied locally and has a soft-top cab which can be clearly be seen here moving straw. (*Vic Morrison*)

6

BRADFORDS IN MUSEUMS AROUND THE WORLD

The Bradford Industrial Museum

The Bradford Industrial Museum has a large collection of Jowetts ranging from 1920s models right up to the post-war Javelin and Jupiter. They also display several Bradfords including a bare chassis and an ultra-rare Bradford ice cream van. It is a fascinating museum and well-worth a visit.

Ray Win Collection New Zealand

Ray Win was a remarkable man who worked with and collected Jowetts for all of his working life and into retirement right up to his death aged 91. He had just finished restoring a CD Bradford which is displayed in the Ray Win Museum along with a very large collection of other Jowetts. One of our club members, Keith Wear, wrote an obituary for Ray for our club magazine, *The Jowetteer*, in June 2012, which reads:

> Club member Ray died on 15th May at his home, aged 91. His continuous connection with Jowetts goes back 64 years to 1948. One year after buying an old blacksmith's shop in Richmond and redeveloping the site as his own small repair garage, he was appointed as Jowett sales and service agent for the northern area of New Zealand's South Island, around Nelson and Marlborough. Not only did he carry out this function well, but he imported Bradford chassis with scuttle and screen, and built Jowett vans and lorries. He had success developing sales of Javelins and Jupiters until Jowett Cars Ltd ceased production. He subsequently took on other agencies whilst still servicing Jowetts for customers and maintaining his own vehicles.

Bradfords in Museums around the World

A 1948 CB chassis registered KTB 520, part of the extensive collection of Jowetts on display in The Bradford Industrial Museum.

This 1949 Bradford ice cream van registered LAT141 was owned by the Guazzelli family in Hull, where it was in service until 1976, it was then acquired by the museum.

This is a 1951 CC Bradford lorry registered KRM 163, it was donated to the museum by the late Keith Dyson, who was a Jowett Car Club member.

This 1951 6-light utility was bought by Frank Smith in 1957, on his death in 1977 his widow donated it to the museum.

Bradfords in Museums around the World

This 1953 CC Bradford van was bought by a Jowett enthusiast in 1984 with only 11,000 miles on the clock, he won the concours award at the Jowett Car Club international rally in Paignton with it in 1985. It was later bought by the museum and is now pained in their 'house colours' and logo.

This early CB Bradford van registered XS6783 is on display in the Scarborough Fair Museum in Scarborough.

Amazingly, The Streetlife Museum in Hull also has a Bradford ice cream van on display, as they are extremely rare, I can only think of five of them. What is even more surprising is that it was in service along with LAT 141 which now lives in the Bradford Industrial Museum!

This continued until the business was sold, but the connection with Jowetts continued and indeed strengthened during retirement. They became a major focus of his life. The mechanical knowledge, bodybuilding skills and love for the marque was combined with his dedication. This resulted in many years spent in restoring over a dozen pre and post-war Jowetts. He formed the Ray Win Collection Community Trust and developed a new building in Nelson to store and display this unique collection of roadworthy vehicles. With additional memorabilia it has become THE place for classic car enthusiasts to visit. The New Zealand Jowett Car Club held their Annual Rally in Nelson in April and all members had the opportunity to visit and view the collection. It was very sad that Ray was unable to welcome them due to having been admitted to hospital at that time, though later he was able to come home. The passing of this remarkable man is the end of an era, but his legacy through the Trust ensures Jowetts in New Zealand will remain for present and future generations.

Ray was a gentleman that I wish I had had the pleasure to meet, as he did more than anybody I know in keeping the Jowett marque alive… NS.

Bradfords in Museums around the World

The Win Collection in New Zealand houses what is probably the largest Jowett collection in the world. These two Bradfords are standing in front of the purpose-built building which houses the collection which covers the whole Jowett range including pre-war models as well as the post-war Javelin, Jupiter and Bradford, including the only restored CD Bradford in the world. (*NZ Classic Driver magazine*)

This is a 1952 Bradford CC utility, known as a station wagon in New Zealand, registered SG911. The yellow truck next to it is described as a 1997 CC model, as it was built by Ray in 1997 out of some of the stock of Jowett spares he was holding. (*NZ Classic Driver magazine*)

This is a 1950 CB Bradford 'Woody' registered NP3965, or 'shooting brake' as we would call it in the UK. The red vehicle at the back with its bonnet open is the only restored CD Bradford in the world at the present time. (*NZ Classic Driver magazine*)

This 1951 CC Bradford van, registered CT3706, has an unusual body built in New Zealand with just one window in the side, with a low tailgate and open above. (*NZ Classic Driver magazine*)

Above: This very attractive 1950 CC lorry, registered DW4559, was delivered to New Zealand as a rolling chassis and was bodied by a local coachbuilder in Christchurch. (*NZ Classic Driver magazine*)

Below left: The Packard Motor Museum in Whangarei, New Zealand has two Bradfords at the moment, they are both in a poor state of repair, but it is hoped that they will be restored one day. This is a 1952 CC example. It carries chassis number KD/E2/ CC/900, which confirms it was a Knock-Down model. This means it was shipped to New Zealand by the Jowett factory in a crate and assembled over there. It also has two different registration plates ET 4238 at the front and HP8225 at the rear—I am assuming that the registration number system may have changed at some time. (*Packard Motor Museum*)

Below right: The second Bradford in the Packard Motor Museum is a 1951 example and carries chassis number E1/CC/33251 its registration number is JM8543. (*Packard Motor Museum*)

Above: The British Car Museum in Hawkes Bay, Te Awanga, New Zealand also have two Bradfords, this one is in the Sanatorium Health Food Company livery. It is clearly a utility with the advertising logos covering the side windows. (*The British Car Museum*)

Below: The second Bradford appears to be another example that has been bodied in New Zealand, the curved waistline that drops away at the rear which lends itself ideally to a two-tone colour scheme. (*The British Car Museum*)

7

A Selection of other Bradfords not covered in the Owners Today Section

There are so many more interesting Bradfords in the UK at the moment, I feel it is appropriate to illustrate a few more of them here after various people's personal accounts of Bradford ownership.

The 1953 Utility registered OYA912 of Paul & Sue Rennie parked next to its elder brother—a 1935 Standard Saloon redgistered BHN334 owned by Roy & Anne Sumpner. The cars were parked outside the RAF Cranford Museum—one of the stops on the 2019 Jowett rally based in Grantham.

Frank Grounds Ltd was the agent for Jowett in Birmingham, he bought several rolling chassis' from the Jowett factory which he built shooting brake bodies for. This 1948 example is thought to be the only survivor. It was bought in the late 1980s by his son, David, who has restored it to a very high standard.

This superb Bradford lorry attended the Jowett Car Club in Peebles in May 2017, it had been driven over from Finland by its owner, Jorma Heikkila, a journey that took several days—needless to say he won the long distance award for attending the rally that year!

A Selection of more Bradfords around Today

Dennis Goode has been a stalwart of the Jowett Car Club for many years and was the Bradford registrar for a considerable time. This is his 1952 six-light CC pictured at the Club's centenary rally in Bingley in 2010.

This 1948 CB lorry is owned by Bob and Joan Dyson and is seen here attending the June 2015 RNLI Flag Weekend in Whitby

This 1948 Bradford lorry was owned by club member Colin Dennison; this picture was taken in April 2013 when it was still owned by Eric Firth. I have used this picture as it is still in this very attractive livery today and is a better picture than my later ones!

Alan Noble has owned The Cyprus Garage in Thackley, Bradford for over 40 years. He has also had these two 1950 CC lorries for a considerable time. *Courtesy Alan Noble*

A Selection of more Bradfords around Today

This is a 1948 CB utility. It is pictured here at the North Yorkshire Moors Railway vintage vehicle rally in July 2007 parked next to my 1952 Jowett Jupiter.

This is an early example, being a 1947 CB owned by Cicely Barker, it was photographed at the Jowett Car Club rally in Daventry in 2011. It also graced the Jowett Car Club stand at the 2013 NEC Classic Car Show in November 2013.

This lovely Bradford was owned by the late Michael Booth, who sadly died in March 2018. He was a real Jowett enthusiast and worked at the Bradford Industrial Museum as a volunteer for many years. He was a real gentleman and is sadly missed.

This Bradford, registered VJY 437 was seen by me for the first time at the Croft Nostalgia Weekend in August 2015. I have chosen a side-view of it to show off its wonderful livery to the best effect.

8

A Celebration of Pictures taken of Bradfords During 2018

It has been a busy year for the Bradford in 2018, a real coming-of-age for the model, here are a few more pictures taken by me at various events with Bradfords in attendance during the year.

A 1952 Bradford van on display at the Former Jowett Employees Rally at the Bradford Industrial Museum in August 2018.

A trio of Bradfords at the Steeple Grange Light Railway, Wirksworth which was the first venue we visited on the Bradford-only rally in May. *Left to right:* JPO 827 Tim Brown, GET 898 Barbara Atack and AEN 853 David Mason.

The 1947 CB lorry of Glyn & Dianne Davies registered CVG 166 at the Steeple Grange Light Railway at Wirksworth, 2018, this was the first outing the Bradford made after its restoration. Dianne has been our club secretary for several years.

A Selection of Pictures Taken of Bradfords during 2018

The second stop on the Bradford-only rally, 2018, was the the Ecclesbourne Railway where this line-up of eight Bradfords made a wonderful display.

The following day the Bradfords visited the The Crich Tramway Museum, here are a trio of Bradfords as part of our display. *Left to right*: FAK 464 Richard Rhodes, GKU 954 Paul Beaumont and GET 898 Barbara Atack.

A line-up of five Bradfords taken at another location at The Crich Tramway Museum, 2018, with Harry Larcombe's 'Bay View Books' Bradford PYB 365 at the rear.

Over the late May bank holiday, 2018, it was the Jowett Car Club international rally where fourteen Bradfords were booked-in. This trio of Bradfords were on display outside the Majestic Hotel, our rally headquarters for the event. *Left to right:* BCW 144 Sara & Rachel Young, OYA 912 Paul & Sue Rennie and FAK 464 Richard Rhodes.

A Selection of Pictures Taken of Bradfords during 2018

This is the 1950 Bradford lorry of Richard Turner and Sarah Eagle registered UMY 564 in the Valley Gardens in Harrogate on the concours day, 2018. This was also the first time out for this vehicle after a full restoration.

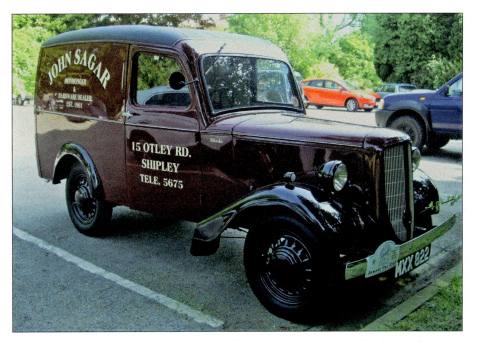

The 1952 CC van of Richard Meekings registered MXX 822 in the Majestic Hotel car park, 2018, it was the first time I had seen this one.

A Selection of Pictures Taken of Bradfords during 2018

This very sad derelict Bradford has recently been discovered in India, where many had been exported to. The owner is employing professional car restorers, Kapur's Vintage Cars, to bring it back from the brink. Most of the rear panels are missing but it is their intention to make it into a 'Woody' shooting brake.

Opposite above: The part-restored Bradford lorry of Alan Bartlett on display at the Bristol Classic Car Show in June 2018, rubbing shoulders with lots of other much shinier vehicles. It did however create a considerable amount of interest!

Opposite below: The Jowett Car Club has held an ex-employee's rally at the Bradford Industrial Museum for over thirty years. This year was the 33rd event which was held on 11 August 2018 where about a dozen old Jowett workers were in attendance together with about 50 Jowetts. There were at least six Bradfords on display, including DUN 825 which is an early 1947 CA model but no longer has its side lights fitted.

Select Bibliography and Acknowledgements

The Autocar magazine

The Motor magazine

Commercial Motor magazine

The Autojumbler magazine

The Jowett Car Club—*The Jowetteer* magazine

Classic & Sportscar magazine

Classic Van & Pick-Up magazine

New Zealand Classic Driver magazine

Old Motor magazine

The Caravan Club

The Telegraph & Argus

Henshall, Andrew, editor of *By Jove!* magazine (JCC Victoria Section, Australia)

Morrison, Vic, editor of *Flat Four* magazine (JCC New Zealand)

The Francis Frith Collection for permission to use the image reference number Y12044

The Packard Motor Museum, State Highway 14, Maungatapere, Whangarei, New Zealand

The British Car Museum, Hawkes Bay, Te Awanga, New Zealand

Clark, Paul, & Nankivell, Edmund, *The Complete Jowett History* (Haynes)

Ebzery, Bill, *The Wait And See Odyssey* (Wait And See Pty Ltd)

Nixon, Allan M., *Beaut Utes 4* by (Penguin)

All photos, unless otherwise stated, are from the author's collection.

SELECT BIBLIOGRAPHY AND ACKNOWLEDGEMENTS

Other titles published by Noel Stokoe:

Jowett 1901-1954 (Images of Motoring), ISBN 10 0-7524-1723-1
My Car was a Jowett, ISBN 10 0-7524-2796-0
Jowett—Advertising the Marque, ISBN 10 0-7524-3535-3
Sporting Jowetts, ISBN 13 978-0-7524-4775-9
Jowett—A Century of Memories, ISBN 13 978-1-4456-0087-1
Jowett's of the 1920's, ISBN 13 978-1-4456-1429-8
Jowett Cars of the 1930's, ISBN 13 978-1-78155-576-7
Journeys Around Whitby, ISBN 13 978-1-4456-4637-4

I would like to take this opportunity to thank my wife, Jane, for her continued support in all my literary efforts relating to Jowett cars—it is greatly appreciated. I would also like to thank my three children, Jonathan—who runs my Facebook and Twitter accounts named MyCarWasAJowett for me—Jessica, and Ben, who have grown up with Jowetts over the last thirty-five years, and also my son-in-law, Liam, who has supported me in all things motoring. Also, to my grandchildren, Luke, Daisy, Oliver, Alexander, Jack, Thomas and Charlie—all 'Jowett Juniors' whom I hope will take up the Jowett cause in the future. Last, but not least, to my many friends in The Jowett Car Club and also locally, who have helped me considerably keeping my cars on the road.

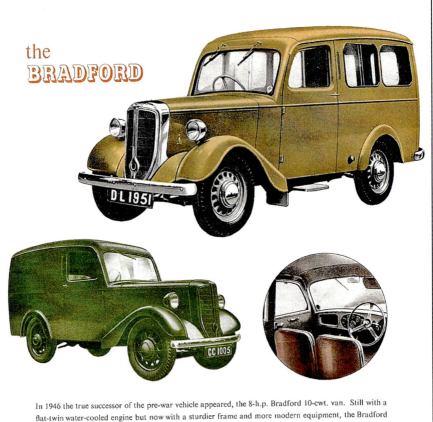

In 1946 the true successor of the pre-war vehicle appeared, the 8-h.p. Bradford 10-cwt. van. Still with a flat-twin water-cooled engine but now with a sturdier frame and more modern equipment, the Bradford quietly got into line production and offered economy, long life, and simplicity to the thousands of tradesmen whom the war had deprived of transport.

Later in the year the Bradford Utility and the lorry appeared, primarily for the export market, whilst at home, having learned by experience or by repute of its economy and reliability, very large numbers of would-be buyers placed their orders, most of them to wait for delivery for a very lengthy period. Early Bradfords did astonishing things. By 1948 one in Canada had covered 150,000 miles with a minimum of maintenance; in early 1947 one covered the arduous Sahara/Congo route to Capetown, and Australia was developing special bodies of great variety to deal with conditions on the big farms. Sweden, Belgium, and the Argentine found these 8-h.p. vehicles capable of the hardest jobs.

Page 9

A page featuring the Bradford range taken from a Jowett publication called *50 Years of Progress – Jowett Cars 1901–1951*.